M000083791

BEHOLD!

The Lamb of God

Kyle Butt & Eric Lyons

Apologetics Press, Inc.
230 Landmark Drive
Montgomery, Alabama 36117-2752

ISBN-10: 0932859933
ISBN-13: 9780932859938
Printed in China

Library of Congress Cataloging-in-Publication
Kyle Butt (1976 -) and Eric Lyons (1975 -)
Behold! The Lamb of God
Includes bibliographic references.
ISBN-10: 0932859933
ISBN-13: 9780932859938
1. Apologetics & Polemics. 2. Jesus Christ & His family. 3. Bible
I. Title

239–dc22 2006923830

DEDICATION

To the faithful parents of our loving wives—Rick & Marilyn Glass and Duane & Joyce Johnson—we dedicate this book about our Lord whom we all serve with joy.

TABLE OF CONTENTS

FOREWORD

Wars come and go. Battles are won and lost. Businesses are bought and sold. Nations rise and fall. Scientific discoveries are made on a daily basis. These and other pertinent events influence human history in a myriad of interesting ways. But none of them is as influential as a powerful personality. Real history is written in names: Napoleon, Stalin, Hitler, Gandhi, Marx, Washington, Lincoln. After all, it is people who make wars, start businesses, forge new nations and cause their collapse. The events instigated by people are by-products of their personalities interacting with their surroundings, other people, and their ideas. In all of human history, one name, one man, has risen to the top of every list of influential personalities—Jesus Christ.

Because of His influence, the life and teachings of Jesus Christ have been more closely scrutinized than any life in human history. This scrutiny has resulted in a number of different reactions. Some have approached a study of His life with an attitude of skepticism, only to arrive on the other side of their spiritual and intellectual journey as firm believers in the deity of Christ. Still others have viewed the life of Jesus as a fictitious myth that deserves no more careful attention than Cinderella or Snow White. A number of people have chosen middle ground in which they acknowledge that Jesus was an amazing teacher and a good man, but they deny that He was the Son of God. And probably the most common response to the life of Jesus is simple apathy. The majority of the billions of people who have lived since the time of Jesus have approached His life neither intently nor earnestly. They have not bothered to discover Who He was and what He did. They have given little attention to the details of His life or His death. What they have heard in passing has been shrugged off without diligent study. Sadly, if most people who have lived since the death of Jesus Christ were asked what they thought about Jesus, they would have to respond, "I don't know. I've never really given Him much thought."

It is high time that the person of Jesus is given His rightful place in the forefront of every person's mind. In the following pages you will be faced with evidence that proves that Jesus was a historical figure, fulfilled prophecies made hundreds of years before He lived, worked legitimate miracles, was resurrected from the grave after His death, and claimed to be the Son of God. You will be forced to answer the question that Jesus posed to His listeners almost 2,000 years ago: "What do you think about the Christ? Whose Son is He?" (Matthew 22:42). Your answer to that question will alter the course of your life for eternity.

CHAPTER 1

THE HISTORICAL CHRIST–
FACT OR FICTION?

Most children and adults can easily recognize the name of Jesus Christ. Many even can recount the story of His life. Also easily recognizable are the names of Peter Pan, Hercules, and Rumpelstiltskin. And most people can relate the "facts" of these fairy tales as well. Is Jesus of Nazareth a fictional character who deserves to be included in a list containing mystifying magicians, daring dragon slayers, and flying boy heroes? The denominational preacher-turned-atheist Dan Barker answered with a resounding "yes" when he wrote:

> The Gospel stories are no more historic than the Genesis creation accounts are scientific. They are filled with exaggerations, miracles, and admitted propaganda. They were written during a context of time when myths were being born, exchanged, elaborated, and corrupted, and they were written to an audience susceptible to such fables. They are cut from the same cloth as other religions and fables of the time. **Taking all of this into account, it is rational to conclude that the New Testament Jesus is a myth** (1992, p. 378, emp. added).

Dan Barker is not the only skeptic to voice opposition to the idea of a historical Jesus. Timothy Freke and Peter Gandy opined:

> We have become convinced that the story of Jesus is not the biography of a historical Messiah, but a myth based on perennial Pagan stories. Christianity was not a new and unique revelation but actually a Jewish adaptation of the ancient Pagan Mystery religion. **This is what we have called The Jesus Mysteries Thesis**... (1999, p. 2, emp. in orig.).

Along the same line of thought, skeptic Marshall J. Gauvin wrote: "Not only has the divinity of Christ been given up, but his existence as a man is being more and more seriously questioned. Some of the ablest scholars of the world deny that he ever lived at all" (1995-2005). In early 2006, an Italian atheist even sued a Catholic priest simply for teaching that Jesus Christ lived on Earth 2,000 years ago (see Lyman, 2006; Owen, 2006).

Is such a view based upon historical evidence and therefore worthy of serious consideration? Or does it represent merely wishful thinking on the part of those who prefer to believe—for whatever reason—that Christ never lived? Was Jesus Christ a man Whose feet got dirty and Whose body grew tired just like the rest of humanity? Fortunately, such questions can be answered by an honest appeal to the available historical evidence.

What is a "historical" person? Martin Kähler suggested: "Is it not the person who originates and bequeaths a permanent influence? He is one of those dynamic individuals who intervene in the course of events" (1896, p. 63). Concerning the historicity of Christ, the skeptic Marshall Gauvin correctly noted, "The question is—what does history say? And that question must be settled in the court of historical criticism.

If the thinking world is to hold to the position that Christ was a real character, there must be sufficient evidence to warrant that belief" (1995-2005). Do sufficient records exist to document the claim that Jesus Christ "intervened in the course of events" known as world history? Indeed, they do.

HOSTILE TESTIMONY

Interestingly, the first type of records comes from what are known commonly as "hostile" sources—writers who mentioned Jesus in a negative light or derogatory fashion. Such penmen certainly were not predisposed to further the cause of Christ or otherwise to add credence to His existence. In fact, quite the opposite is true. They rejected His teachings and often reviled Him as well. Thus, one can appeal to them without the charge of built-in bias.

In his book, *The Historical Figure of Jesus*, E.P. Sanders stated: "Most of the first-century literature that survives was written by members of the very small elite class of the Roman Empire. To them, Jesus (if they heard of him at all) was merely a troublesome rabble-rouser and magician in a small, backward part of the world" (1993, p. 49, parenthetical comment in orig.). It is now to this "small elite class of the Roman Empire" that we turn our attention for documentation of Christ's existence.

Tacitus

Tacitus (c. A.D. 56-117) should be among the first of several hostile witnesses called to the stand. He was a member of the Roman provincial upper class with a formal education who held several high positions under different emperors such as Nerva and Trajan (see Tacitus, 1952, 15:7). His famous work, *Annals*, was a history of Rome written in approximately A.D. 115. In the *Annals* he told of the Great Fire of Rome, which occurred in A.D. 64. Nero, the Roman emperor in office at the time, was suspected by many of having ordered the city set on fire. Tacitus wrote:

> Nero fabricated scapegoats—and punished with every refinement the notoriously depraved Christians (as they were popularly called). Their originator, Christ, had been executed in Tiberius' reign by the governor of Judea, Pontius Pilatus. But in spite of this temporary setback the deadly superstition had broken out afresh, not only in Judea (where the mischief had started) but even in Rome (1952, 15.44, parenthetical comments in orig.).

Tacitus hated both Christians and their namesake, Christ. He therefore had nothing positive to say about what he referred to as a "deadly superstition." He did, however, **have something to say about it.** His testimony establishes beyond any reasonable doubt that the Christian religion not only was relevant historically, but that Christ, as its originator, was a verifiable historical figure of such prominence that He even attracted the attention of the Roman emperor himself!

Suetonius

Additional hostile testimony originated from Suetonius, who wrote around A.D. 120. Robert Graves, as translator of Suetonius' work, *The Twelve Caesars*, declared:

> Suetonius was fortunate in having ready access to the Imperial and Senatorial archives and to a

> great body of contemporary memoirs and public documents, and in having himself lived nearly thirty years under the Caesars. Much of his information about Tiberius, Caligula, Claudius, and Nero comes from eye-witnesses of the events described (Suetonius, 1957, p. 7).

The testimony of Suetonius is a reliable piece of historical evidence. In his history, Suetonius wrote: "Because the Jews at Rome caused continuous disturbance at the instigation of Chrestus, he [Claudius—KB/EL] expelled them from the city" (*Claudius*, 25:4; note that in Acts 18:2 Luke mentioned this expulsion by Claudius). Sanders commented that *Chrestus* is a probable misspelling of *Christos*, "the Greek word that translates the Hebrew 'Messiah' " (1993, pp. 49-50). Suetonius further noted: "Punishments were also inflicted on the Christians, a sect professing a new and mischievous religious belief" (*Nero*, 16:2). Again, it is evident that Suetonius and the Roman government had feelings of hatred toward this mischievous band of rebels.

Pliny the Younger

Along with Tacitus and Suetonius, Pliny the Younger must be allowed to take a seat among hostile Roman witnesses. In approximately A.D. 110-111, Pliny was sent by the Roman emperor Trajan to govern the affairs of the region of Bithynia. From this region, Pliny corresponded with the emperor concerning a problem he viewed as quite serious. He wrote: "Having never been present at any trials of the Christians, I am unacquainted with the method and limits to be observed either in examining or punishing them" (*Letters*). He then went on to state:

> In the meanwhile, the method I have observed towards those who have been denounced to me as Christians is this: I interrogated them whether they were Christians; if they confessed it I repeated the question twice again, adding the threat of capital punishment; if they still persevered, I ordered them to be executed (*Letters*).

Pliny used the term "Christian" or "Christians" seven times in his letter, thereby corroborating it as a generally accepted term that was recognized by both the Roman Empire and its emperor. Pliny also used the name "Christ" three times to refer to the originator of the "sect." He noted that those who had professed Christianity

> affirmed, however, the whole of their guilt, or their error, was, that they were in the habit of meeting on a certain fixed day before it was light, when they sang in alternate verses a hymn to Christ, as to a god, and bound themselves by a solemn oath, not to any wicked deeds... (*Letters*).

It is undeniably the case that Christians, with Christ as their founder, had multiplied in such a way as to draw the attention of the emperor and his magistrates by the time of Pliny's letter to Trajan. In light of this evidence, it is impossible to deny the fact that Jesus Christ existed and was recognized by the highest officials within the Roman government as an actual, historical person.

Some have attempted to negate the testimony of these hostile Roman witnesses to Christ's historicity by suggesting that the "Roman sources that mention him are all dependent on Christian reports" (Sanders, 1993, p. 49). For example, in his book, *The Earliest Records of Jesus*, Francis Beare lamented:

> Everything that has been recorded of the Jesus of history was recorded for us by men to whom he was Christ the Lord; and we cannot expunge their faith from the records without making the records themselves virtually worthless. There is no Jesus known to history except him who is depicted by his followers as the Christ, the Son of God, the Saviour to the World (1962, p. 19).

Such a suggestion is as outlandish as it is outrageous. Not only is there no evidence to support such a claim, but all of the available evidence militates against it. Furthermore, it is an untenable position to suggest that such upper class Roman historians would submit for inclusion in the official annals of Roman history (to be preserved for posterity) facts that were related to them by a notorious tribe of "mischievous," "depraved," "superstitious" misfits.

Even a casual reader who glances over the testimony of the hostile Roman witnesses who bore testimony to the historicity of Christ will be struck by the fact that these ancient men depicted Christ as neither the Son of God nor the Savior of the world. They verbally stripped Him of His Sonship, denied His glory, and belittled His magnificence. They described Him to their contemporaries, and for posterity, as a mere man. Yet even though they were wide of the mark in regard to the truth of **Who** He was, through their caustic diatribes they nevertheless documented **that** He was. And for that we are indebted to them.

TESTIMONY OF JESUS AMONG THE JEWS

Even though much of the hostile testimony regarding the existence of Jesus originated from witnesses within the Roman Empire, such testimony is not the only kind of hostile historical evidence available. Anyone familiar with Jewish history will recognize immediately the *Mishnah* and the *Talmud*. The *Mishnah* was a book of Jewish law traditions codified by Rabbi Judah around the year A.D. 200 and known to the Jews as the "whole code of religious jurisprudence" (Bruce, 1960, pp. 100-102). Jewish rabbis studied the *Mishnah* and even wrote a body of commentary based upon it known as the *Gemaras*. The *Mishnah* and *Gemares* are known collectively as the *Talmud* (Bruce, 1960, p. 100-102). The complete *Talmud* surfaced around A.D. 300. If a person as influential as Jesus had existed in the land of Palestine during the first century, surely the rabbis would have had **something** to say about him. Undoubtedly, a man who supposedly confronted the most astute religious leaders of His day—and won—would be named among the opinions of those who shared His rabbinical title. As Bruce declared:

> According to the earlier Rabbis whose opinions are recorded in these writings, Jesus of Nazareth was a transgressor in Israel, who practised magic, scorned the words of the wise, led the people astray, and said that he had not come to destroy the law but to add to it. He was hanged on Passover Eve for heresy and misleading the people. His disciples, of whom five are named, healed the sick in his name (1953, p. 102).

Bruce's quote sums up several of the thoughts taken from the Jewish writings known as the *Sanhedrin Tractate*, in which the Jewish leaders wrote: "On the eve of the Passover Yeshu was hanged. For forty days before the execution took place, a herald went forth and cried, 'He is going forth to be stoned because he has practiced sorcery and enticed Israel to apostacy.... But since nothing was brought forward in his favour he was hanged on the eve of Passover" (Shachter, 43a). [Note: *Yeshu* or *Yeshua* is the Hebrew spelling equivalent to the name Jesus.]

First-century Judaism, in large part, refused to accept Jesus Christ as the Son of God. Yet it did not refuse to accept Him as a historical man from a literal city known as Nazareth, or to record for posterity crucial facts about His life and death.

Josephus

Josephus is another important Jewish witness. The son of Mattathias, he was born into a Jewish upper class priestly family around A.D. 37. His education in biblical law and history stood among the best of his day (Sanders, 1993, p. 15). At age nineteen, he became a Pharisee. When Jerusalem rebelled against the Roman authorities, he was given command of the Jewish forces in Galilee. After losing most of his men, he surrendered to the Romans. He found favor in the man who commanded the Roman army, Vespasian, by predicting that Vespasian soon would be elevated to the position of emperor. Josephus' prediction came true at Vespasian's inauguration in A.D. 69. After the fall of Jerusalem, Josephus assumed the family name of the emperor (Flavius) and settled down to live a life as a government pensioner. It was during these latter years that he wrote *Antiquities of the Jews* between September 93 and September 94 (Bruce, 1960, pp. 102-104). Josephus himself gave the date as the thirteenth year of Domitian (Rajak, 1984, p. 237). His contemporaries viewed his career indignantly as one of traitorous rebellion to the Jewish nation (Bruce, 1960, p. 103).

Twice in *Antiquities*, Jesus' name flowed from Josephus' pen. *Antiquities* 18:3:3 reads as follows:

> And there arose about this time Jesus, a wise man, *if indeed we should call him a man*; for he was a doer of marvelous deeds, a teacher of men who receive the truth with pleasure. He led away many Jews, and also Greeks. *This man was the Christ.* And when Pilate had condemned him to the cross on his impeachment by the chief men among us, those who had loved him at first did not cease; *for he appeared to them on the third day alive again, the divine prophets having spoken these and thousands of other wonderful things about him*: and even now the tribe of Christians, so named after him, has not yet died out (italics added).

Certain historians regard the italicized segments of the section as "Christian interpolation." There is, however, no evidence from textual criticism that would warrant such an opinion (Bruce, 1953, p. 110). In fact, every extant Greek manuscript contains the disputed portions. The passage also exists in both Hebrew and Arabic versions. And although the Arabic version is slightly different, it still exhibits knowledge of the disputed sections (see Chapman, 1981, p. 29; Habermas, 1996, pp. 193-196).

There are several reasons generally offered for rejecting the passage as genuine. First, early Christian writers like Justin Martyr, Tertullian, and Origen did not use Josephus' statement in their defense of Christ's deity. Habermas observed that Origen, in fact, documented the fact that Josephus (although himself a Jew) did not believe Christ to be the Messiah (1996, p. 192;

cf. Origen's *Against Celsus*, 1:47). However, as Habermas also pointed out, the fourth-century writer Eusebius, in his *Ecclesiastical History* (1:11), quoted Josephus' statement about Christ, including the disputed words. And he undoubtedly had access to much more ancient sources than those now available.

Furthermore, it should not be all that surprising that such early Christian apologists did not appeal to Josephus in their writings. Wayne Jackson has suggested:

> Josephus' writings may not have been in extensive circulation at that point in time. His *Antiquities* was not completed until about 93 A.D. Too, in view of the fact that Josephus was not respected by the Jews, his works may not have been valued as an apologetic tool (1991b, 11:29).

Such a suggestion possesses merit. Professor Bruce Metzger commented: "Because Josephus was deemed a renegade to Judaism, Jewish scribes were not interested in preserving his writings for posterity" (1968, p. 75). Thomas H. Horne, in his *Critical Introduction to the Study and Knowledge of the Holy Scriptures*, referred to the fact that the main source of evidence frequently used by the so-called "church fathers" was an appeal to the Old Testament rather than to human sources (1841, 1:463-464). The evidence substantiates Horne's conclusion. For example, a survey of the index to the eight volumes of the multi-volume set, *The Ante-Nicene Fathers*, reveals only eleven references to Josephus in the entire set.

The second reason sometimes offered as to why the disputed passage in Josephus' *Antiquities* might be due to "Christian interpolation" is the fact that it seems unlikely that a non-Christian writer would include such statements as "this man was the Christ" or "if indeed we should call him a man." But while such might be unlikely, it certainly is not beyond the realm of possibility. Any number of reasons could explain why Josephus would write what he did. For example, Bruce allowed for the possibility that Josephus might have been speaking sarcastically (1953, p. 110). Howard Key suggested:

> If we assume that in making explicit statements about Jesus as Messiah and about the resurrection Josephus is merely conveying what Jesus' followers claimed on his behalf, then there would be no reason to deny that he wrote them [i.e., the supposed interpolated phrases—KB/EL] (1970, p. 33).

It also should be noted that Josephus hardly qualifies as the sole author of such statements made about Christ by those who rejected His deity. Ernest Renan, for example, was a nineteenth-century French historian whose book, *The Life of Jesus*, was a frontal assault on Christ's deity that received major attention throughout Europe (see Thompson, 1994, 14:5). Yet in that very volume Renan wrote: "This sublime person, who each day still presides over the destiny of the world, we may call divine.... In him was condensed all that is good and elevated in our nature" (n.d.).

Or consider H.G. Wells who, in 1931, authored *The Outline of History*. On page 270 of that famous work, Wells referred to Jesus as "a prophet of unprecedented power." No one who knew Wells (a man who certainly did not believe in the divinity of Christ) ever would accuse his account of being flawed by "Christian interpolation." The famous humanist, Will Durant, was an avowed atheist, yet he wrote: "The greatest question of our time is not communism vs. individualism, not Europe vs. America, not even the East vs. the West; it is whether men can bear to live without God" (1932, p. 23). Comments like those of Renan, Wells, and Durant document the fact that, on occasion, even unbelievers have written complimentary about God and Christ.

Furthermore, even if the material containing the alleged Christian interpolation is removed, the vocabulary and grammar of the section "cohere well with Josephus' style and language" (Meier, 1990, p. 90). In fact, almost every word (omitting for the moment the supposed interpolations) is found elsewhere in Josephus (Meier, p. 90). Were the disputed material to be expunged, the testimony of Josephus still would verify the fact that Jesus Christ actually lived. Habermas therefore concluded:

> There are good indications that the majority of the text is genuine. There is no textual evidence against it, and, conversely, there is very good manuscript evidence for this statement about Jesus, thus making it difficult to ignore. Additionally, leading scholars on the works of Josephus [Daniel-Rops, 1962, p. 21; Bruce, 1967, p. 108; Anderson, 1969, p. 20] have testified that this portion is written in the style of this Jewish historian (1996, p. 193).

In addition, Josephus did not remain mute regarding Christ in his later sections. *Antiquities* 20:9:1 relates that Ananus brought before the Sanhedrin "a man named James, the brother of Jesus who was called the Christ, and certain others. He accused them of having transgressed the law, and condemned them to be stoned to death." Bruce observed that this quote from Josephus "is chiefly important because he calls James 'the brother of Jesus the so-called Christ,' in such a way as to suggest that he has already made reference to Jesus. And we do find reference to him in all extant copies of Josephus" (Bruce, 1953, p. 109). Meier, in an article titled "Jesus in Josephus," made it clear that rejecting this passage as actually having been written by Josephus defies accurate assessment of the text (pp. 79-81). Meier also added another emphatic defense of the historical reliability of the text in *Antiquities* concerning Christ.

> Practically no one is astounded or refuses to believe that in the same book 18 of *The Jewish Antiquities* Josephus also chose to write a longer sketch of another marginal Jew, another peculiar religious leader in Palestine, "John surnamed the Baptist" (*Ant.* 18.5.2). Fortunately for us, Josephus had more than a passing interest in marginal Jews (p. 99).

Even skeptic Jeffrey Jay Lowder, the "co-founder and past President of Internet Infidels, Inc., an international coalition of nontheists dedicated to promoting and defending a naturalistic worldview on the Internet," after attempting to refute much of the historical evidence regarding Jesus, had this to say concerning the testimony of Josephus: "I think there is ample evidence to conclude there was a historical Jesus. To my mind, the New Testament alone provides sufficient evidence for the historicity of Jesus, **but the writings of Josephus also provide two independent, authentic references to Jesus**" (2000, emp. added).

The simple fact is that this well-educated, Jewish historian wrote about a man named Jesus Who actually existed in the first century. Yamauchi summarized quite well the findings of the secular sources regarding Christ:

> Even if we did not have the New Testament or Christian writings, we would be able to conclude from such non-Christian writings as Josephus, the *Talmud*, Tacitus and Pliny the Younger that: (1) Jesus was a Jewish teacher; (2) many people believed that he performed healings and exorcisms; (3) he was rejected by the Jewish leaders; (4) he was crucified under Pontius Pilate in the reign of Tiberius; (5) despite this shameful death, his followers, who believed that he was still alive, spread beyond Palestine so that there were multitudes of them in Rome by 64 A.D.; (6) all kinds of people from the cities and countryside—men and women, slave and free—worshiped him as God by the beginning of the second century (1995, p. 222).

EARLY PATRISTIC WRITERS

Early patristic writers compose one significant group of witnesses to the historicity of Christ that should not be overlooked. This group of men lived and composed writings from the end of the first century to the eighth century A.D. Although their writings are admittedly Christian in their orientation, the early date of many of the writings provides excellent evidence for the historicity of Christ.

For instance, Polycarp, an early Christian who lived from approximately A.D. 69-155, wrote several letters, including one titled *The Epistle to the Philippians*. In this epistle, he mentions Jesus at least eleven times, explains that Jesus "suffered even unto death," and quotes several commandments and remarks from Jesus (n.d.). Irenaeus, another early patristic writer who lived from approximately A.D. 120-202, noted several interesting things about Polycarp, when he wrote:

> For I have a more vivid recollection of what occurred at that time than of recent events...so that I can even describe the place where the blessed Polycarp used to sit and discourse—his going out, too, and his coming in—his general mode of life and personal appearance, together with the discourses which he delivered to the people; also how he would speak of his familiar intercourse with John, and with the rest of those who had seen the Lord; and how he would call their words to remembrance. Whatsoever things he had heard from them respecting the Lord, both with regard to His miracles and His teaching, Polycarp having thus received [information] from the eyewitnesses of the Word of life, would recount them all in harmony with the Scriptures (Irenaeus, n.d.).

A host of other early church writers can be documented and referenced along similar lines. Origen lived from about A.D. 185-253, Justin Martyr from 100-165, Tertullian from 160-215, and Clement of Alexandria from 150-215. Each of these men, and others from comparable time periods, wrote extensively about Christ, the church He established, and Christians. Their writings offer added testimony to the historicity of Christ. (For more extensive reading about the early patristic writers and their actual writings, see Knight, 2004.)

CHAPTER 2

RELIABILITY OF THE NEW TESTAMENT RECORDS

Although the list of hostile, Jewish, and early patristic witnesses proves beyond the shadow of a doubt that Jesus actually lived, it is by no means the only historical evidence available to those interested in this topic. The gospel accounts (Matthew, Mark, Luke, and John), and the other 23 books that form the New Testament, provide more information about Jesus than any other source(s) available. But may these records be viewed as historical evidence, or are they instead writings whose reliability pales in comparison to other types of historical documentation? Blomberg has explained why the historical question of the gospel accounts, for example, must be considered.

> Many who have never studied the gospels in a scholarly context believe that biblical criticism has virtually disproved the existence [of Christ—KB/EL]. An examination of the gospel's historical reliability must therefore precede a credible assessment of who Jesus was (1987, p. xx).

But how well do the New Testament documents compare with additional ancient, historical documents? F.F Bruce examined much of the evidence surrounding this question in his book, *The New Testament Documents–Are They Reliable?* (1967). As he and other writers have noted (e.g., Metzger, 1968, p. 36; Geisler and Brooks, 1990, p. 159), there are over 5,300 manuscripts of the Greek New Testament in existence today, in whole or in part, that serve to corroborate the accuracy of the New Testament. [NOTE: According to Michael Welte of the Institute for New Testament Textual Research in Munster, Germany, the number of Greek manuscripts in **2005**—whole and partial—stood at 5,748 (Welte, 2005).] The best manuscripts of the New Testament are dated at roughly A.D. 350, with perhaps one of the most important of these being the Codex Vaticanus, "the chief treasure of the Vatican Library in Rome," and the Codex Sinaiticus, which was purchased by the British from the Soviet Government in 1933 (Bruce, 1953, p. 20). Additionally, the Chester Beatty papyri, made public in 1931, contain eleven codices, three of which contain most of the New Testament (including the gospel accounts). Two of these codices boast of a date in the first half of the third century, while the third slides in a little later, being dated in the last half of the same century (Bruce, 1953, p. 21). The John Rylands Library boasts of even earlier evidence. A papyrus codex containing parts of John 18 dates to the time of Hadrian, who reigned from A.D. 117 to 138 (Bruce, 1953, p. 21).

Other attestation to the accuracy of the New Testament documents can be found in the writings of the so-called "apostolic fathers"—men who wrote primarily from A.D. 90 to 160 (Bruce, 1953, p. 22). Irenaeus, Clement of Alexandria, Tertullian, Tatian, Clement of Rome, and Ignatius (writing before the close of the second century) all provided citations from one or more of the gospel accounts (Guthrie, 1990, p. 24). Other witnesses to the early authenticity of the New Testament are the ancient versions, which consist of the text of the New Testament translated into different languages. The Old Latin and the Old Syriac are the most ancient, being dated from the middle of the second century (Bruce, 1953, p. 23).

The available evidence makes it clear that the gospel accounts were accepted as authentic by the close of the second century (Guthrie, p. 24). They were complete before A.D. 100, with many of the writings circulating 20-40 years before the close of the first century (Bruce, 1953, p. 16). Linton remarked:

> A fact known to all who have given any study at all to this subject is that these books were quoted, listed, catalogued, harmonized, cited as authority by different writers, Christian and Pagan, right back to the time of the apostles (1943, p. 39).

Such an assessment is absolutely correct. In fact, the New Testament enjoys far more historical documentation than any other volume ever known. There are only 643 copies of Homer's *Iliad*, which is undeniably the most famous book of ancient Greece. No one doubts the text of Julius Caesar's *Gallic Wars*, but we have only 10 copies of it, the earliest of which was made 1,000 years after it was written. To have such abundance of copies for the New Testament from within 70 years of their origination is nothing short of amazing (Geisler and Brooks, 1990, pp. 159-160).

Someone might allege that the New Testament documents cannot be trusted because the writers had an agenda. But this in itself does not render what they said untruthful, especially in the light of corroborating evidence from hostile witnesses. There are other histories that are accepted despite their authors' agendas. An "agenda" does not nullify the possibility of accurate historical knowledge.

In his work, *The New Testament Documents–Are They Reliable?*, Bruce offered more astounding comparisons. Livy wrote 142 books of Roman history, of which a mere 35 survive. The 35 known books are made manifest due to some 20 manuscripts, only one of which is as old as the fourth century. We have only two manuscripts of Tacitus' *Histories* and *Annals*, one from the ninth century and one from the eleventh. The *History of Thucydides*, another well-known ancient work, is dependent upon only eight manuscripts, the oldest of these being dated about A.D. 900 (along with a few papyrus scraps dated at the beginning of the Christian era). *The History of Herodotus* finds itself in a similar situation. "Yet no classical scholar would listen to an argument that the authenticity of Herodotus or Thucydides is in doubt because the earliest MSS of their works which are of any use to us are over 1,300 years later than the originals" (Bruce, 1953, pp. 20-21). Bruce thus declared: "It is a curious fact that historians have often been much readier to trust the New Testament records than have many theologians" (1953, p. 19). As Linton put it:

> There is no room for question that the records of the words and acts of Jesus of Galilee came from the pens of the men who, with John, wrote what they had "heard" and "seen" and their hands had "handled of the Word of life" (1943, pp. 39-40).

FACTUAL ACCURACY OF THE NEW TESTAMENT DOCUMENTS

The New Testament does not necessarily claim to be a systematic representation of first-century history. It is not, per se, merely a history book. It does claim, however, that the historical facts related in the text are accurate, with no margin of error (2 Timothy 3:16-17; Acts 1:1-3). It is safe to say that, due to this extraordinary claim, the New Testament has been scrutinized more intensely than any other text in existence (with the possible exception of its companion volume, the Old Testament). What has been the end result of such scrutiny?

The overwhelming result of this close examination is an enormous cache of amazing archaeological evidence that testifies to the exactitude of the various historical references in the New Testament. As can be said of virtually every article on archaeology and the Bible, the following few pages that document this archaeological evidence only scratch the surface of the available evidence. Nevertheless, an examination of this particular subject makes for a fascinating study in biblical accuracy. If the New Testament records can be proven to be factually accurate in every checkable case, then their testimony regarding Jesus must be accepted as accurate and legitimate as well.

The Pilate Inscription

Few who have read the New Testament accounts of the trial of Jesus can forget the name Pontius Pilate. All four gospel accounts make reference to Pilate. His inquisition of Jesus, at the insistence of the Jewish mob, stands as one of the most memorable scenes in the life of Jesus. No less than three times, this Roman official explained to the howling mob that he found no fault with Jesus (John 18:38; 19:4,6). Wanting to placate the Jews, however, Pilate washed his hands in a ceremonial attestation to his own innocence of the blood of Christ, and then delivered the Son of God to be scourged and crucified.

What can be gleaned from secular history concerning Pilate? For approximately 2,000 years, the only references to Pilate were found in such writings as Josephus and Tacitus. The written record of his life placed him as the Roman ruler over Judea from A.D. 26-36. The records indicate that Pilate was a very rash, often violent man. The biblical record even mentioned that Pilate had killed certain Galileans while they were presenting sacrifices (Luke 13:1). Besides an occasional reference to Pilate in certain written records, however, there were no inscriptions or stone monuments that documented his life.

Such remained the case until 1961. In that year, Pilate moved from a figure who was known solely from ancient literature, to a figure who was attested to by archaeology. The Roman officials who controlled Judea during Jesus' time, most likely made their headquarters in the ancient town of Caesarea, as evinced from two references by Josephus to Pilate's military and political activity in that city (Finegan, 1992, p. 128). Located in Caesarea was a large Roman theater that a group of Italian-sponsored archaeologists began to excavate in 1959. Two years later, in 1961, researchers found a two-foot by three-foot slab of rock that had been used "in the construction of a landing between flights of steps in a tier of seats reserved for guests of honor" (see McRay, 1991, p. 204). The Latin inscription on the stone, however, proved that originally, it was not meant to be used as a building block in the theater. On the stone, the researchers found what was left of an inscription bearing the name of Pontius Pilate. The entire inscription is not legible, but concerning the name of Pilate, Finegan remarked: "The name Pontius Pilate is quite unmistakable, and is of much importance as the first epigraphical documentation concerning Pontius Pilate, who governed Judea A.D. 26-36 according to commonly accepted dates" (1992, p. 139). What the complete inscription once said is not definitely known, but there is general agreement that originally the stone may have come from a temple or shrine dedicated to the Roman emperor Tiberius (Blaiklock, 1984, p. 57). A stronger piece of evidence for the New Testament's accuracy would be difficult to find. Now known appropriately as "The Pilate Inscription," this stone slab documents that Pilate was the Roman official governing Judea, and even uses his more complete name of Pontius Pilate, as found in Luke 3:1.

Politarchs in Thessalonica

When writing about the Christians in Thessalonica who were accused of turning "the world upside down," Luke noted that some of the brethren had been brought before the "rulers of the city" (Acts 17:5-6). The phrase "rulers of the city" (NKJV, ASV; "city authorities"—NASB) is translated from the Greek word *politarchas*, and occurs only in Acts 17 verses 6 and 8. For many years, critics of the Bible's claim of divine inspiration accused Luke of a historical inaccuracy because he used the title *politarchas* to refer to the city officials of Thessalonica, rather than employing the more common terms, *strateegoi* (magistrates) or *exousiais* (authorities). To support their accusations, they pointed out that the term *politarch* is found nowhere else in Greek literature as an official title. Thus, they reasoned that

Luke made a mistake. How could someone refer to such an office if it did not exist? Whoever heard or read of *politarchas* in the Greek language? No one in modern times. That is, no one in modern times had heard of it until it was found recorded in the various cities of Macedonia—the province in which Thessalonica was located.

In 1960, Carl Schuler published a list of 32 inscriptions bearing the term *politarchas.* Approximately 19 out of the 32 came from Thessalonica, and at least three of them dated back to the first century (see McRay, 1991, p. 295). On the Via Egnatia (a main thoroughfare through ancient Thessalonica), there once stood a Roman Arch called the Vardar Gate. In 1867, the arch was torn down and used to repair the city walls (p. 295). An inscription on this arch, which is now housed in the British Museum, ranks as one of the most important when dealing with the term *politarchas.* This particular inscription, dated somewhere between 30 B.C. and A.D. 143, begins with the phrase, "In the time of Politarchas..." (Finegan, 1959, p. 352). Thus, the arch most likely was standing when Luke wrote his historical narrative known as Acts of the Apostles. And the fact that politarchs ruled Thessalonica during the travels of Paul now stands as indisputable.

Sergius Paulus the Proconsul of Cyprus

Throughout the apostle Paul's missionary journeys, he and his fellow travelers came in contact with numerous prestigious people—including Roman rulers of the area in which the missionaries were preaching. If Luke had been fabricating these travels, he could have made vague references to Roman rulers without giving specific names and titles. But that is not what one finds in the book of Acts. On the contrary, it seems that Luke went out of his way to document specific cities, places, names, and titles. Because of this copious documentation, we have ample instances in which to check his reliability as a historian.

One such instance is found in Acts 13. In that chapter, Luke documented Paul's journey into Seleucia, then Cyprus and Salamis, then Paphos. In Paphos, Paul and his companions encountered two individuals—a Jew named Bar-Jesus and Sergius Paulus, an intelligent man who summoned Paul and Barnabas in order to hear the Word of God (Acts 13:4-7). This particular reference to Sergius Paulus provides the student of archaeology with a two-fold test of Luke's accuracy. First, was the area of Cyprus and Paphos ruled by a proconsul during the time of Paul's work there? Second, was there ever a Sergius Paulus?

For many years, skeptics of Luke's accuracy claimed that the area around Cyprus would not have been ruled by a proconsul. Since Cyprus was an imperial province, it would have been put under a "propraetor," not a proconsul (Unger, 1962, pp. 185-186). While it is true that Cyprus at one time had been an imperial province, it is not true that it was such during Paul's travels there. In fact, "in 22 B.C. Augustus transferred it to the Roman Senate, and it was therefore placed under the administration of proconsuls" (Free and Vos, 1992, p. 269). Biblical scholar F.F. Bruce expanded on this information when he explained that Cyprus was made an imperial province in 27 B.C., but that Augustus gave it to the Senate five years later in exchange for Dalmatia. Once given to the Senate, proconsuls would have ruled Cyprus, just as in the other senatorial provinces (Bruce, 1990, p. 295). As Thomas Eaves remarked:

> As we turn to the writers of history for that period, Dia Cassius (*Roman* History) and Strabo (*The Geography of Strabo*), we learn that there were two periods of Cyprus' history: first, it was an imperial province governed by a propraetor, and later in 22 B.C., it was made a senatorial province governed by a proconsul. Therefore, the historians support Luke in his statement that Cyprus was ruled by a proconsul, for it was between 40-50 A.D. when Paul made his first missionary journey. If we accept secular history as being true we must also accept Biblical history, for they are in agreement (1980, p. 234).

In addition to the known fact that Cyprus became a senatorial province, archaeologists have found copper coins from the region that refer to other proconsuls who were not much removed from the time of Paul. One such coin, called appropriately a "copper proconsular coin of Cyprus," pictures the head of Claudius Caesar, and contains the title of "Arminius Proclus, Proconsul...of the Cyprians" (McClintock and Strong, 1968, 2:627).

Even more impressive than the fact that Luke had the specific title recorded accurately, is the fact that evidence has come to light that the record of Sergius Paulus is equally accurate. It is interesting, in this regard, that there are several inscriptions that possibly could match the proconsul recorded by Luke. The *International Standard Bible Encyclopedia* (ISBE) records three ancient inscriptions that could be possible matches (see Hughes, 1986, 2:728). First, at Soli on the north coast of Cyprus, an inscription was uncovered that mentioned Paulus, who was a proconsul. The authors and editors of the *ISBE* contend that the earliest this inscription can be dated is A.D. 50, and that it therefore cannot fit the Paulus of Acts 13. Others, however, are convinced that this is the Paulus of Acts' fame (Unger, 1962, pp. 185-186; see also McGarvey, n.d., *New Commentary...*, 2:7). In addition to this find, another Latin inscription has been discovered that refers to a Lucius Sergius Paulus who was "one of the curators of the Banks of the Tiber during the reign of Claudius." Eminent archaeologist Sir William Ramsay argued that this man later became the proconsul of Cyprus, and should be connected with Acts 13 (Hughes, 2:728). Finally, a fragmentary Greek inscription hailing from Kythraia in northern Cyprus has been discovered that refers to a Quintus Sergius Paulus as a proconsul during the reign of Claudius (Hughes, 2:728). Regardless of which of these inscriptions actually connects to Acts 13, the evidence provides a plausible match. At least two men named Paulus were proconsuls in Cyprus, and at least two men named Sergius Paulus were officials during Claudius' reign. Luke's accuracy is confirmed once again.

Gallio, Proconsul of Achaia

Acts chapter 18 opens with a description of Paul's ministry in the city of Corinth. It was there that he came into contact with Aquila and his faithful wife Priscilla, both of whom had been expelled from Rome at the command of Claudius (cf. Suetonius, *Claudius*, 25:4), and who, as a result, had come to live in Corinth. Because they were tentmakers, like Paul, the apostle stayed with them and worked as a "vocational minister," making tents and preaching the Gospel. As was usually the case with Paul's preaching, many of the Jews were offended, and opposed his work. Because of this opposition, Paul told the Jews that from then on he would go to the Gentiles. That said, Paul went to the house of a man named Justus who lived next door to the synagogue. Soon after his proclamation to go to the Gentiles, Paul had a vision in which the Lord instructed him to speak boldly, because no one in the city would attack him. Encouraged by the vision, Paul continued in Corinth for a year and six months, teaching the Word of God among the people.

After Paul's eighteen-month-long stay in Corinth, the opposition to his preaching finally erupted into violent, political action. Acts 18:12-17 explains.

> When Gallio was proconsul of Achaia, the Jews with one accord rose up against Paul and brought him to the judgment seat, saying, "This fellow persuades men to worship God contrary to the law." And when Paul was about to open his mouth, Gallio said to the Jews, "If it were a matter of wrongdoing or wicked crimes, O Jews, there would be reason why I should bear with you. But if it is a question of words and names and your own law, look to it yourselves; for I do not want to be a judge of such matters." And he drove them from the judgment seat. Then all the Greeks took Sosthenes, the ruler of the synagogue, and beat him before the judgment seat. But Gallio took no notice of these things.

From this brief pericope of Scripture, we learn several things about Gallio and his personality. Of paramount importance to our discussion is the fact that Luke recorded that Gallio was the "proconsul of Achaia."

Here again Luke, in recording specific information about the political rulers of his day, provided his readers with a checkable point of reference. Was Gallio ever really the proconsul of Achaia?

Marianne Bonz, the former managing editor of the *Harvard Theological Review*, shed some light on a now-famous inscription concerning Gallio. She recounted how, in 1905, a doctoral student in Paris was sifting through a collection of inscriptions that had been collected from the Greek city of Delphi. In these various inscriptions, he found four different fragments that, when put together, formed a large portion of a letter from the Emperor Claudius. The letter from the emperor was written to none other than Gallio, the proconsul of Achaia (Bonz, 1998, p. 8).

McRay, in giving the Greek portions of this now-famous inscription, and supplying missing letters in the gaps of the text to make it legible, translated it as follows:

> Tiberius Claudius Caesar Augustus Germanicus, Pontifex Maximus, of tribunician authority for the twelfth time, imperator twenty-sixth time.... Lucius Junius Gallio, my friend, and the proconsul of Achaia (1991, pp. 226-227).

While certain portions of the above inscription are not entirely clear, the name of Gallio and his office in Achaia are clearly legible. Not only did Luke accurately record the name of Gallio, but he likewise recorded his political office with equal precision.

The importance of the Gallio inscription goes even deeper than verification of Luke's accuracy. This particular find shows how archaeology can give us a better understanding of the biblical text, especially in areas of chronology. Most scholars familiar with the travels and epistles of the apostle Paul will readily admit that attaching specific dates to his activities remains an exceedingly difficult task. The Gallio inscription, however, has added a small piece to this chronological puzzle. Jack Finegan, in his detailed work on biblical chronology, dated the inscription to the year A.D. 52, Gallio's proconsulship in early A.D. 51, and Paul's arrival in Corinth in the winter of A.D. 49/50. Finegan stated concerning his conclusion: "This determination of the time when Paul arrived in Corinth thus provides an important anchor point for the entire chronology of Paul" (1998, pp. 391-393).

Over and over, biblical references that can be checked, prove to be historically accurate in every detail. After hundreds of years of critical scrutiny, both the Old and New Testaments of the Bible have proven their authenticity and accuracy at every turn. Sir William Ramsay, in his assessment of Luke's writings in the New Testament, wrote:

> You may press the words of Luke in a degree beyond any other historian's, and they stand the keenest scrutiny and the hardest treatment, provided always that the critic knows the subject and does not go beyond the limits of science justice (1915, p. 89).

Today, almost a hundred years after that statement originally was written, the exact same thing can be said with even more certainty of the writings of Luke—and every other Bible writer. The documentation of the life of Jesus Christ as a historical fact by the New Testament records stands as one of the greatest attestations to any historical fact in the entire course of human history.

CONCLUSION

When someone asks the question, "Is the life of Jesus Christ a historic event?," he or she must remember that "[i]f we maintain that the life of our Lord is not a historical event, we are landed in hopeless difficulties; in consistency, we shall have to give up all ancient history and deny that there ever was such an event as the assassination of Julius Caesar" (Monser, 1961, p. 377). And, we will have to deny the historical reliability of the New Testament documents.

Faced with such overwhelming evidence, it is unwise to reject the position that Jesus Christ actually walked the streets of Jerusalem in the first century. As Harvey has remarked, there are certain facts about Jesus that "are attested by at least as much reliable evidence as are countless others taken for granted as historical facts known to us from the ancient world." But lest we be accused of misquoting him, let us point out that Harvey went on to say, "It can still be argued that we can have no reliable historical knowledge about Jesus with regard to anything that really matters" (1982, p. 6).

Harvey could not deny the fact that Jesus lived on this Earth. Critics do not like having to admit it, but they cannot successfully deny the fact that Jesus had a greater impact on the world than any single life before or after. Nor can they deny the fact that Jesus died at the hands of Pontius Pilate. Harvey and others can say only that such facts "do not really matter." We contend that the facts that establish the existence of Jesus Christ of Nazareth really **do** matter. As Bruce stated, "The earliest propagators of Christianity welcomed the fullest examination of the credentials of their message" (1953, p. 122). While Paul was on trial before King Agrippa, he said to Festus: "For the king, before whom I also speak freely, knows these things; for I am convinced that none of these things escapes his attention, since this thing was not done in a corner" (Acts 26:26).

As the earliest apologists of Christianity welcomed a full examination of the credentials of the message that they preached, so do we today. These credentials have been weighed in the balance and **not** found wanting. The simple fact of the matter is that Jesus Christ did exist and lived among men.

> It is impossible to say that no one has the right to be an agnostic. But no one has the right to be an agnostic till he has thus dealt with the question, and faced this fact with an open mind. After that, he may be an agnostic—if he can (Anderson, 1985, p. 12).

CHAPTER 3

JESUS CHRIST—UNIQUE SAVIOR OR AVERAGE FRAUD?

The freshman college student walked into his first class of *Comparative Religions 101.* He had come to the university prepared—or so he thought—for whatever college might throw at him. After all, he was a faithful Christian, and had been reared by dedicated Christian parents who, throughout his upbringing, had taught him about the unique, heaven-sent, virgin-born, miracle-working, resurrected-from-the-dead Son of God that he revered, served, and loved. His Bible class teachers, and the ministers to whose sermons he had listened for the past eighteen years, similarly had reinforced in his mind the concept that there was **no one** in the entire history of the world quite like Jesus Christ. In fact, truth be told, the young student had grown up thinking that no one even came close to resembling, or imitating, the carpenter's son from Nazareth.

This young student, however, was about to receive the shock of his life. From the first day of class, the professor began to recite a host of similar stories about various "saviors" of other religions from the past—many of whom, supposedly, also were born of virgins, were able to perform miracles, were crucified to save mankind, and were resurrected after their deaths. This freshman was ill prepared to hear his professor suggest that **the story of Jesus Christ as the Savior of**

mankind is not totally unique. In fact, he was completely astonished as he watched the professor document the fact that stories with similar heroes had circulated for decades—and even centuries—before Jesus of Nazareth was born. As he saw what he believed to be the uniqueness of His Lord essentially evaporate before his very eyes, the young man began to wonder: Had he been taught incorrectly? Was Jesus **really** the unique Son of God, or was He simply one among many characters of the past who **claimed** to be a unique, personal savior but who, in the end, was not? Who were these other allegedly "unique saviors"? Were they as distinctive as they, or their followers, claimed? And how do such claims impact the Bible's teachings about, and a person's individual faith in, Jesus Christ as the Son of God?

During his struggle to cope with the new information that was being presented so eloquently (and so forcefully!) by his professor, this young man encountered what is known as "cognitive dissonance"—the confusion one experiences when presented with new information that contradicts what he or she believes to be true. As he struggled for consistency, the young man realized that he either had to abandon what he believed to be true, or somehow disprove (and thereby discount) the new, challenging information.

The more he thought about the matter, the more likely—and unsettling—the first option seemed to become. And the more impossible the second seemed to appear. Left unchecked, his struggle would reach the level of full-blown doubt, and his confidence in the singular uniqueness of the Savior he had loved and obeyed for so long would disappear completely.

How could he be helped—or could he? Was the material to which he was being exposed trustworthy? Or could it be refuted—thus leaving his personal faith in Christ intact? The answers to these questions form the basis of our study in this chapter.

WHO ARE THESE OTHER "UNIQUE SAVIORS"?

History is filled with examples of those whose lives—real or imagined—share certain traits with the well-documented life of Jesus of Nazareth. Such accounts often compose a portion of the curriculum in college-level comparative religion courses, and provide a fine starting point for any study about the uniqueness of Jesus.

Consider, for example, Dionysus, a well-known, mythological god. The usual story of his birth relates that he was the offspring of Zeus, the immortal leader of the Greek gods who impregnated a human female by the name of Semele, the daughter of Cadmus, King of Thebes (see Graves, 1960, p. 56). Dionysus is said to have descended to the underworld and conquered death, ultimately bringing his dead mother back to the land of the living. He also is said to have died and been raised again. His followers called him Lysios or *Redeemer*, and grape juice was commonly used to symbolize his blood. As one writer noted: "Many Christians would be horrified to think that Jesus is in some way a manifestation of Dionysus, but the parallels are complex and deep.... Like Jesus, Dionysus is a god whose tragic passion is re-enacted by eating his flesh and drinking his blood" ("Dionysus and Yeshua," n.d.).

The Dionysus cult reached Rome in 496 B.C., but had been around long before that. The similarities in the accounts of Dionysus and Jesus (as well as in that of Osiris, the Egyptian god of fertility and ruler of the underworld, discussed below)—from their unique births, to their resurrections, to their lives being commemorated in a similar fashion by their followers—are striking, indeed. In fact, in their 1999 book, *The Jesus Mysteries,* Timothy Freke and Peter Gandy discussed at length such similarities in support of the idea that the Jesus of Christianity never existed, but in fact was little more than a mythological character of antiquity. They wrote:

> The more we studied the various versions of the myth of Osiris-Dionysus, the more it became obvious that the story of Jesus had all the characteristics of this perennial tale. Event by event, we found we were able to construct Jesus' supposed biography from mythic motifs previously related to Osiris-Dionysus:
>
> Osiris-Dionysus is God made flesh, the savior and "Son of God."
>
> His father is God and his mother is a mortal virgin.
>
> He is born in a cave or humble cowshed on December 25 before three shepherds.
>
> He offers his followers the chance to be born again through the rites of baptism.
>
> He miraculously turns water into wine at a marriage ceremony.
>
> He rides triumphantly into town on a donkey while people wave palm leaves to honor him.
>
> He dies at Eastertime as a sacrifice for the sins of the world.

> After his death he descends to hell, then on the third day he rises from the dead and ascends to heaven in glory.
>
> His followers await his return as the judge during the Last Days.
>
> His death and resurrection are celebrated by a ritual meal of bread and wine, which symbolize his body and blood.
>
> These are just some of the motifs shared between the tales of Osiris-Dionysus and the biography of Jesus. Why are these remarkable similarities not common knowledge? (p. 5).

Dionysus hardly is the only character from the past whose life supposedly parallels that of Jesus. Consider Krishna, the ancient Hindu deity who is alleged to have shared a doom similar to Christ's. He has been portrayed as hanging on a cross, with holes through his hands and his feet. His title?—"Our Lord and Savior." Krishna supposedly "rose from the dead" and then "ascended bodily into heaven" (Doane, 1882, p. 215). He even is purported to have said: "Do good for its own sake, and expect not your reward for it on Earth" (Graves, 1875, p. 112). Christ employed the same idea in Matthew 6. But Krishna's story dates to 1200 B.C.

The parallels continue. In the Egyptian *Papyrus of Ani* (also known as *The Egyptian Book of the Dead*), which is dated between 1450 and 1400 B.C. (see Budge, 1960, p. 220), the god Osiris commands the titles of King of Kings, Lord of Lords, and Prince of Princes (Budge, p. 352). In his intriguing book, *Bible Myths and Their Parallels in Other Religions*, T.W. Doane observed: "Osiris, the Egyptian Saviour, after being put to death, **rose from the dead**, and bore the title of '**The Resurrected**

One' " (p. 221, emp. in orig.). Osiris' scribe, Ani, is described as one "whose word is truth" (Budge, p. 384). In the latter part of the papyrus, a specific creed is provided that supposedly is capable of providing justification for the person who recites it upon his or her entrance into eternity. That creed reads as follows: "I have given bread to the hungry man, and water to him that was athirst, and apparel to the naked man, and a ferry-boat to him that had no boat" (Budge, p. 587). The writer of this papyrus could have copied the words of Jesus as found in Matthew 25:31-46—except for one small fact: the *Papyrus of Ani* dates to 1400 B.C.—over a thousand years **before** Christ made His earthly appearance.

Furthermore, in 550 B.C., Confucius said: "Do not to another what you would not want done to yourself." Christ uttered an almost identical statement approximately 600 years **after** Confucius when He said: "And as ye would that men should do to you, do ye also to them likewise" (Luke 6:31).

Similarities also exist between the stories of Buddha and Jesus. In the cover story article he authored for the March 27, 2000 issue of *Newsweek* on "The Other Jesus," Kenneth L. Woodward commented that "the life stories of Jesus and Buddha are strikingly similar," and then went on to note that both of these religious leaders challenged the religious teachings of their day, allegedly were born of virgins, and were supposed to have worked miracles (135[13]:58-59).

Some Bible critics have suggested that it would be a simple matter to cite stories with similarities such as these by the dozen. In fact, in a public debate with theist Norman Geisler (held at Columbus College in

Columbus, Georgia on March 29, 1994), Farrell Till, a former-Christian-turned-skeptic, stated exactly that when he said to the audience:

> People, I want you to stop and think seriously for just a moment. I know how much emotionalism is involved in this, but please understand this. Crucified, resurrected savior-gods, who had been born of virgins, were a dime a dozen at this time (1994).

Stephen Franklin—although an avid defender of Christ's uniqueness—corroborated Till's statement in an article in the *Evangelical Review of Theology* when he wrote: "Incarnation, far from being unique to Christianity, seems to be a universal possession of the religious heritage of mankind" (1993, p. 32).

Christ's critics have used such parallels time and again in an attempt to establish their contention that Jesus of Nazareth is neither a unique character nor a worthy, personal savior. For example, three weeks after Kenneth Woodward's article on Jesus was published in *Newsweek*, a letter to the editor from Don Zomberg of Wyoming, Michigan appeared in the April 20 edition of the magazine. In response to a quotation from Woodward's article which suggested that "Christ is absolutely original and absolutely unique," Mr. Zomberg wrote to dissent when he said: "Nothing could be further from the truth. The legend of Jesus is little more than a variant of older religions common to the Middle East thousands of years ago" (2000, 135 [16]:17). Such an attitude—which stems from the fact that historical and mythological parallels between Jesus and other religious personalities **do** exist—likely is much more prevalent than many people realize. And while it is true that none of these historical/mythological parallels is **exact**, it is true that some are close enough to elicit serious investigation on the part of those who believe Jesus Christ to be the unique Son of God.

Of course, contemporary skeptics who use such an argument in attempts to debunk the uniqueness and deity of Christ cannot take credit as its originators. History records that almost two thousand years ago the early Christian apologists were busily engaged in responding to the exact same argument. For example, Augustine of Hippo (A.D. 354-426) stated in his *Christian Doctrine*:

> The readers and admirers of Plato dared calumniously to assert that our Lord Jesus Christ learnt all those sayings of His, which they are compelled to admire and praise, from the books of Plato—because (they urged) it cannot be denied that Plato lived long before the coming of our Lord (n.d., 2:28, parenthetical item in orig.).

Augustine refuted the argument by suggesting that Plato had read the prophet Jeremiah and then conveniently incorporated Jeremiah's teachings into his own. The point, however, is clear: as early as A.D. 400, skeptics and enemies of the cross were launching fiery darts of alleged plagiarism at both Christ and His followers.

Further investigation into the history of Christian apologetics manifests something even more startling. The earliest apologists not only recognized that the story and teachings of Jesus bore striking similarities to ancient mythological accounts, but even **emphasized these similarities** in an attempt to get pagans to understand more about Jesus and His mission. Justin Martyr (A.D. 100-165) set forth an argument in his *First Apology* that was intended to put Christ at least on an equal playing field with earlier mythological gods.

> And if we assert that the Word of God was born of God in a peculiar manner, different from ordinary generation, let this, as said above, be no extraordinary thing to you, who say that Mercury is the angelic word of God. But if any one objects that He was crucified, in this also He is on a par with those reputed sons of Jupiter of yours.... And if we even affirm that He was born of a virgin, accept this in common with what you accept of Ferseus. And in that we say that He made whole the lame, the paralytic, and those born blind, we seem to say what is very similar to the deeds said to have been done by Æsculapius (Chapter 22).

Tertullian (c. A.D. 160-220) observed that the story of Romulus, another character from ancient Greek mythology who was seen after his death, was quite similar to the story of Christ being seen after His death. However, Tertullian went on to note that the stories of Christ were much more certain because they were documented by historical evidence (*Apology,* 21).

While ancient pagans saw, and modern skeptics still see, such similarities as militating against the originality and uniqueness of Christ, the writings of such men as Augustine, Justin Martyr, Tertullian, and others document the fact that early Christians could see obvious—yes, even welcome—similarities between the story of Jesus and the accounts of mythological, pagan gods. Furthermore, some of those early Christians even seized upon those very similarities to defend Jesus' position as the unique Son of God. The apologists' point, of course, was two-fold: (1) men of the past **had** searched for a unique savior-god and, finding none, resorted to inventing him and bestowing upon him certain distinct characteristics; and (2) that Savior—who, although in the past had been endowed with unique traits of their own feeble creation—actually **had come**!

Christians need to recognize as an undeniable fact—a fact confirmed by mythology, history, and even early Christian apologists—that ancient documents reveal that the story of Christ is not the first story ever told of a virgin-born, crucified, resurrected, miracle-working savior-god who supposedly died for the sins of humanity. These documents further reveal that many of Christ's teachings can be gleaned—at times almost verbatim—from sources that were in circulation hundreds or thousands of years before Jesus was born. Early apologists acknowledged these facts because they were, and are, quite indisputable.

And that leads us back to the issue that plagued the college freshman mentioned earlier. How, in light of such facts, can we affirm that Jesus Christ is the unique, authentic Son of God—when stories similar to His circulated decades or millennia before He ever came to Earth? What response can we offer to the Bible critics' charges? And what assurance may we offer to the young student about the genuineness of his faith?

WHY AN UNORIGINAL JESUS?

Before we address whether or not Jesus is the actual Savior, the obvious question must be asked: Why would anyone **want** to claim that the story of Jesus is unoriginal or plagiaristic? There probably are several answers that could be offered to such an inquiry. Due to space restrictions, however, let us concentrate on only two. First, it is a simple fact that those who do not believe in God, and who consequently accept a completely naturalistic view of the origin of the Universe and its inhabitants, must find **some** way to explain the uniqueness of Christ and the uniqueness of the system of religion He instituted. In addressing this point, the late James Bales wrote:

> If one accepts a naturalistic and evolutionary account of the origin of religion, he will believe that Christianity can be explained naturally. His very approach has ruled out the possibility of the supernatural revelation of God in Jesus Christ (n.d., p. 7).

Eminent British evolutionist Sir Julian Huxley asserted:

> In the evolutionary pattern of thought there is no longer need or room for the supernatural. The earth was not created; it evolved. So did all the animals and plants that inhabit it, including our human selves, mind, and soul as well as brain and body. **So did religion** (1960, pp. 252-253, emp. added).

Those who believe that the Universe and life within it evolved in a purely naturalistic fashion likewise must find a totally naturalistic cause for **every** facet of life. Religion itself is one of those facets, and therefore, according to the naturalist, also must have evolved—exactly as Huxley suggested it did. It is not difficult to see why an evolutionist would believe it to be inevitable that the story of Jesus originated from earlier, primitive stories. In fact, to say that the story of Jesus "evolved" from older, more primitive stories is to assert nothing more than what the theory of evolution already teaches in every other area of human existence. Atheist Joseph McCabe explained: "What we see, in fact, is **evolution in religion**. The ideas pass on from age to age, a mind here and a mind there adding or refining a little. The slow river of human evolution had entered its rapids" (1926, p. 72, emp. added).

Second, while some may be motivated by a search for a purely naturalistic origin of religion, others teach that the story of Jesus is derived from earlier Jewish and/or pagan myths and legends. As Bales went on to observe, some have suggested that "Christ and Christianity are viewed as natural developments out of Judaism and paganism" (n.d., p. 7). That very position has been defended by former-believers-turned-apostates, Timothy Freke and Peter Gandy, in *The Jesus Mysteries* (which is an all-out, frontal assault on the divinity of Christ).

> We had both been raised as Christians and were surprised to find that, despite years of open-minded spiritual exploration, it still felt somehow dangerous to even dare think such thoughts. Early indoctrination reaches very deep. We were in effect saying that Jesus was a Pagan god and that Christianity was a heretical product of Paganism! It seemed outrageous. Yet this theory explained the similarities between the stories of Osiris-Dionysus and Jesus Christ in a simple and elegant way. They are parts of one developing mythos....
>
> The Jesus story does have all the hallmarks of a myth, so could it be that that is exactly what it

> is...? Why should we consider the stories of Osiris, Dionysus, Adonis, Attis, Mithras, and the other Pagan Mystery saviors as fables, yet come across essentially the same story told in a Jewish context and believe it to be the biography of a carpenter from Bethlehem?
>
> We have become convinced that the story of Jesus is not the biography of a historical Messiah, but a myth based on perennial Pagan stories. Christianity was not a new and unique revelation but actually a Jewish adaptation of the ancient Pagan Mystery religion. This is what we have called **The Jesus Mysteries Thesis**....
>
> The obvious explanation is that as early Christianity became the dominant power in the previously Pagan world, popular motifs from Pagan mythology became grafted onto the biography of Jesus.... Such motifs were "borrowed" from Paganism in the same way that Pagan festivals were adopted as Christian saints' days.... The Jesus story is a perennial myth...not merely a history of events that happened to someone 2,000 years ago (1999, pp. 9-10,2,6,13, emp. in orig.).

And so, while there actually may have been a literal person known as "Jesus Christ," he was nothing more than that—literally a person. The traits claimed for Him by His followers (e.g., unusual entrance into the world, unusual activities during His pilgrimage on Earth, unusual exit from this world, etc.) arose "after the fact" as a result of having been derived or plagiarized from ancient pagan and/or Jewish sources.

It is not Christ's historicity that is at stake here (which was dealt with in the first chapter); the majority of unbelievers and infidels of every stripe have long acknowledged His existence. Rather, the issue has to do with whether or not Jesus of Nazareth was Who He claimed to be—the unique, "only begotten," incarnate Son of God.

MAN'S RELIGIOUS FACULTY AND "SAVIOR SIMILARITIES"

The truth of the matter is that many stories over the course of history resemble that of Jesus of Nazareth in one way or another. And why should this surprise us? After Adam and Eve ate from the tree of knowledge of good and evil, man became keenly aware of both the presence and the consequences of sin. From the time of Cain and Abel, God had established sacrifices and decreed specific rules regarding those sacrifices. Since that time, all humans have had at least some perception—however slight or flawed—that they needed to "do something" to stand justified once again before their Creator. One way to do that was to invent a "stand-in"—someone who could take their place—as the epitome of sinless perfection to plead their case before the Righteous Judge of all the Earth (cf. Genesis 18:25).

Additionally, however, it can be argued that the similarities we have listed (and, indeed, many others just like them) are **only similarities,** not exact parallels. It further can be argued that Jesus' story, even though it seems similar to some others, is not exactly the same and, in fact, differs substantially in the minute details. For example, Krishna allegedly was crucified via an arrow through his arms, while Jesus was nailed to the cross. Confucius offered the negative form of the so-called "golden rule" ("**Do not** do to others"), while Jesus stated the positive ("**Do** unto others"). Dionysus' mother, Persophone, reportedly had intercourse with Zeus, while Mary was a virgin. This line of reasoning possesses some merit, because it certainly is true that none of the ancient stories sounds **exactly** like Christ's.

A closer look at the Egyptian legend of Osiris provides a good example of the many important differences between the account of Jesus and other stories. Legend says that Osiris was killed by his evil brother Seth, who tore Osiris' body into fourteen pieces and scattered them throughout Egypt. Isis, the goddess-consort of Osiris, collected the pieces and buried them, thus giving life to Osiris in the underworld. Afterward, she used magical arts to revive Osiris and to conceive a child (Horus) by him. After fathering Horus, Osiris remained in the underworld, not really ever rising from the dead ("Osiris," 1997, 8:1026-1027). This legend, taken as a whole, provides few (if any) real parallels to the story of Jesus. Furthermore, when all the stories about characters who supposedly were similar to Christ are told in their entirety, it is obvious that each of them contains only a few characteristics that come anywhere close to resembling those contained in the life story of Jesus.

However, there are some common threads that weave their way through many of the various legends: a superhuman hero does miraculous things, is killed to save mankind (sometimes even by crucifixion), and is brought back to life in some form or another, thereby defeating death. Although the minute details are quite different, the general similarities are close enough to demand scrutiny—and an explanation. As an illustration, suppose someone were to take this copyrighted book, use a thesaurus to change hundreds of its words, and then put his or her name on it without permission. Such a person would be viewed as an obvious plagiarizer. Although the new book might be "unique" in its minutia, in its broad strokes it still would be a copy. In a similar vein, it is not enough for Christians to claim that the story of Jesus did not originate from one (or more) of the hundreds of ancient stories simply by saying that the minute details of His particular life are different from the others. We must offer a better, more thorough, and more convincing argument if the story of Jesus Christ is to be defended as genuinely unique.

Independent Nature of Similar Stories

In the early part of the twentieth century, Joseph McCabe, one of the most outspoken atheists of his day, published several works, including *The Myth of the Resurrection* (1925), *Did Jesus Ever Live?* (1926), and *How Christianity "Triumphed"* (1926). In 1993, Prometheus Publishing Company (note that the title of this secular publishing organization is the name of one of the Greek gods supposedly similar to Jesus) republished these works in a book titled *The Myth of the Resurrection and Other Essays.* McCabe painstakingly documented the similarities between the story of Jesus and pagan stories such as those of Osiris, Adonis, Tammuz, and Attis, yet specifically noted: "It is a most important feature of our story that this legend of a slain and resurrected god **arose in quite different parts of the old civilized world**. Tammuz, Attis, and Osiris are three **separate and independent creations** of the myth-making imagination" (1926, p. 45, emp. added). McCabe thus acknowledged that these pagan stories with similar themes did not copy either one another or some earlier, predominant story. Rather, they arose separately—and even independently—of each other. McCabe admitted: "For some reason...the mind of man came in most parts of the world to conceive a legend of death and resurrection.... In fact, in one form or other there was almost a **worldwide belief** that the god, or a representative [king, prisoner, effigy, etc.] of the god, died, or had to die every year" (pp. 52,53, emp. added; bracketed material in orig.). In his conclusion, McCabe wrote: "In sum, I should say that the **universal belief in a slain and resurrected god** throws light upon the Christian belief by showing us a universal frame of mind which quite easily, in many places, made a resurrection myth" (p. 63, emp. added). McCabe—even as an infidel—willingly acknowledged that numerous (but different) resurrection myths arose from various regions around the globe, each similar in its facts yet original in its derivation. These stories apparently arose because of what he referred to as a "universal frame of mind." And yet in spite of such evidence, on page 69 of his book, McCabe concluded: "**Man has no religious instinct**."

Mankind's Religious Instinct

People around the world—due to a "universal frame of mind"—independently concocted stories that revolved around a god dying and then rising again. These stories span both time barriers and geographical limits; they are—in a very real sense—"worldwide" and "universal." Yet we are asked to believe that the people from different countries and cultures who concocted these stories possessed "no religious instinct"? How McCabe could make the concessions he did, yet reach such a conclusion, defies rational explanation.

In truth, man **does** have a religious instinct—one that is keener than even many theologians would like to admit. In speaking of God, the writer of Ecclesiastes remarked: "He hath made everything beautiful in its time: **he hath set eternity in their heart**" (3:11). Paul said that mankind always has been able to understand God's "everlasting power and divinity" (Romans 1:20 ASV). God did not place man on Earth to abandon him. Instead:

> He made of one every nation of men to dwell on all the face of the earth, having determined their appointed seasons and bounds of their habitation; that they should **seek** God, if haply they might feel after him and find him though he is not far from each one of us; for in him we live, and move and have our being; **as certain of your own poets have said**, for we are his offspring (Acts 17:26-28, emp. added).

God has indeed "set eternity" in the hearts of men and given them a universal instinct that is intended to cause them to seek Him.

In his book, *Why We Believe the Bible,* the late George DeHoff commented: "No nation or tribe has been found which did not believe in a Supreme Being of some kind and practice religion in some form" (1944, p. 42). He is absolutely right. But it is not just believers who have presented and documented this kind of information. Even nonbelievers have been forced to such a conclusion by the historical and scientific evidence.

Over seventy years ago, Clarence Darrow and Wallace Rice joined forces to edit a book titled *Infidels and Heretics: An Agnostic's Anthology*. On the inside cover, a description of the book's contents suggested that it contained "the best gleanings from the most important works of the great agnostics, skeptics, infidels and heretics of the world." On page 146, the compilers quoted the famous skeptic, John Tyndall:

> Religion lives not by the force and aid of dogma, but because it is ingrained in the nature of man. To draw a metaphor from metallurgy, the moulds have been broken and reconstructed over and over again, but the molten ore abides in the ladle of humanity. An influence so deep and permanent is not likely soon to disappear... (1929).

Approximately fifty years later, Edward O. Wilson of Harvard University (who is known as the "father" of the biological discipline of sociobiology) penned a book titled *On Human Nature*. The inside front cover stated that Wilson's goal was "nothing less than the completion of the Darwinian revolution by bringing biological thought into the center of the social sciences and the humanities." Wilson wrote: "The predisposition to religious belief is the most complex and powerful force in the human mind and in all probability an ineradicable part of human nature" (1978, p. 167). He went on to say that "skeptics continue to nourish the belief that science and learning will banish religion, which they consider to be no more than a tissue of illusions," yet the idea that increased learning and technology will strip mankind of his religious nature "has never seemed so futile as today" (p. 170).

PROPHETS OF OLD AND THE PERFECT SACRIFICE

How, then, did the instinct to worship God lead to the concoction of numerous stories about a virgin-born savior-god who dies as a sacrifice for mankind's wrongdoings? First, it started with prophecies about a Redeemer Who would bring salvation to mankind. According to several Bible passages, the prophets of old had been foretelling of a coming Redeemer since the beginning of time. When Jesus rebuked the Pharisees and lawyers for their hypocrisy, He mentioned their unrighteous ancestors and made the following statement:

> Therefore the wisdom of God also said, "I will send them prophets and apostles, and some of them they will kill and persecute," that the blood of all the prophets which was shed **from the foundation of the world** may be required of this generation, **from the blood of Abel** to the blood of Zechariah who perished between the altar and the temple. Yes, I say to you, it shall be required of this generation (Luke 11:49-51, emp. added).

Jesus asserts that God used prophets as far back as "the foundation of the world," specifically from the time of Abel, Adam's second son recorded in Scripture. The apostle Peter made a similar statement while preaching to thousands of Jews in Solomon's Portico.

> Repent therefore and be converted, that your sins may be blotted out, so that times of refreshing may come from the presence of the Lord, and that He may send Jesus Christ, who was preached to you before, whom heaven must receive until the times of restoration of all things,

> **which God has spoken by the mouth of all His holy prophets since the world began** (Acts 3:19-21, emp. added).

"Since the world began," God has revealed messages to mankind via His prophets. Sometimes these messages were regarding the coming physical destruction upon a particular nation (e.g., Jonah 3:1-10; Nahum 1-3). At other times, they were about one particular person or tribe of people (e.g., Genesis 40; 49). But no prophecies were more important (nor more prevalent in Scripture) than those concerning Christ. And, God's spokesmen have been foretelling His Coming specifically **since the earliest of times**. Luke recorded how, after the birth of John the Baptizer, his father, Zacharias, "was filled with the Holy Spirit, and prophesied, saying,"

> Blessed is the Lord God of Israel, for He has visited and redeemed His people, and has raised up a horn of salvation for us in the house of His servant David, as He spoke by the mouth of His holy prophets, who **have been since the world began** (Luke 1:67-70, emp. added).

God's prophets have not foretold the coming of a great Redeemer only since the Mosaic period, nor were prophecies concerning the Savior of the world limited to the Jewish people. Zacharias rejoiced that God was sending the Redeemer and Savior of Whom the prophets had spoken "**since the world began**." Admittedly, most all of the Messianic prophecies recorded in Scripture appear after God revealed to Abraham that through his seed "all the nations of the world shall be blessed" (Genesis 22:18; 12:1-3; 49:10; etc.). Yet, one recorded messianic prophecy goes back centuries before Abraham—all the way to Adam and Eve's tenure in the Garden of Eden. There God informed the serpent following his deception of Eve: "I will put enmity between you and the woman, and between your seed and her Seed; He shall bruise your head, and you shall bruise His heel" (Genesis 3:15). In this very first messianic prophecy, a suffering, but victorious, Redeemer is pictured.

Thousands of years later, hundreds of similar prophecies about the Christ were given to the Israelites. It is logical to conclude, however, that similar messianic prophecies would have been delivered by other prophets outside of Judaism. The patriarch Enoch, just seven generations from Adam, "walked with God three hundred years" and "prophesied" (Genesis 5:22; Jude 14). His great-great-grandson Noah, whom the apostle Peter described as "a preacher of righteousness" (2 Peter 2:5), very likely knew of the Messianic prophecies during patriarchal times, and may very well have received direct revelation from God on the matter (similar to how God spoke to him regarding the Flood—Genesis 6:13-21). Centuries later, non-Jewish, God-fearing men such as Melchizedek, king of Salem, "the priest of the Most High God" (Genesis 14:18; Hebrews 7:1), Job, and others worshiped and served the one true God.

We have no way of knowing how many of God's spokesmen through the centuries have prophesied about the coming of a Savior. We do know, however, that some prophecies about Christ are virtually as old as the world itself, and the Bible nowhere pretends to contain **every** Messianic prophecy **ever** spoken.

One may reasonably conclude that a chief reason nations outside of Israel possessed stories of savior-gods who share many commonalities with Jesus is because **they had heard either inspired prophets foretell the Redeemer's coming, or the prophecies made "from the foundation of the world" had been passed down to them by word of mouth.** Interestingly, some of the first people on Earth to recognize the arrival of the Messiah were men the Bible calls—not Jews—but "wise men (magi, NASB) from the East" (Matthew 2:1). From where did these men receive such knowledge? How did they know that a particular "star in the East" (Matthew 2:2) would indicate the Messiah's entrance into the world? The fact is, they received Divine direction (cf. Matthew 2:1-12).

Truly, God's scheme of redemption through a "hero" that would save the world from sin and death has been revealed since the fall of man. Simply because civilizations from the past (outside of Judaism and Christianity) possessed similar "redemption" stories and/or knowledge of a Redeemer should not be troubling or surprising. They likely were based (at least partly) on messages preached by the prophets of old.

Second, stories about a savior-god were perpetuated by the idea of sacrifice. From the moment Adam and Eve were driven from the Garden of Eden, man was acutely aware that he was a sinful being in need of redemption. Humans also understood that some type of atoning sacrifice was required to absolve them of sin. The writer of the book of Hebrews observed that "by faith Abel offered to God a more excellent sacrifice than Cain" (11:4). Oddly, skeptics seem to understand this point quite well. In the late eighteenth century, T.W. Doane caustically attacked the doctrines of Christ and the Bible. His work, *Bible Myths and Their Parallels in Other Religions* (1882), gnawed at every mooring of Christian doctrine. Yet even he understood that mankind always has realized its own sinfulness and its need for an atoning sacrifice. He wrote: "The doctrine of atonement for sin had been preached long before the doctrine was deduced from the Christian Scriptures, long before these Scriptures are pretended to have been written" (p. 181). Bible scholar R.C. Trench commented:

> Nations in which it is impossible could have learned it from one another, nations the most diverse in culture, the highest in the scale and well nigh the lowest, differing in everything besides, have yet agreed in this one thing, namely, in the offering of things which have life to God,—or, where the idea of the one God has been lost,—to the "gods many" of heathenism—the essential feature of that offering in every case being that the life of the victim was rendered up (n.d., p. 177).

Those who might wish to challenge Trench's assessment can examine any book on world history or world religions and see that he is correct. Mankind has sacrificed living things to a deity from earliest times. Abel offered the first of his flock and since then humanity has been offering sacrifices in the hope of absolving anger and forgiving sin. But which **particular** sacrifices did humanity think had the power to forgive sins? The general rule for the atonement value of a sacrifice was: **the more costly and perfect the sacrifice, the more sins it would absolve.**

When God initiated the ritual sacrifice of animals for the religious ceremonies of His chosen people, He laid down strict rules. In Leviticus 22:19-20, God told the Jews: "You shall offer of your own free will a male without blemish from the cattle, from the sheep, or from the goats. But whatever has a defect, you shall not offer, for it shall not be acceptable on your behalf." The Lord **always** has demanded that blood be shed for the remission of sins. Hebrews 9:22 reiterates that point: "And according to the law almost all things are purified with blood, and without shedding of blood there is no remission." This should not be at all surprising, since "the life of the flesh is in the blood, and I have given it to you upon the altar to make atonement for your souls; for it is the blood that makes atonement for the soul" (Leviticus 17:11).

Men and women of ages past knew all too well God's commandments regarding atonement by blood. It began with Cain and Abel, was reaffirmed by Noah (Genesis 9:1-6), was regulated by Old Testament law, and was carried through to fulfillment by Jesus. When God instituted the Law of Moses, He did not introduce animal sacrifices as an innovation never before seen by the Israelites. Rather, He showed the Israelites the proper manner in which to sacrifice such animals, until the time that the fulfilling sacrifice of His Son would bring to a halt the need for any further blood atonement via animal sacrifices. In showing them the proper way, God made strict provisions to keep the children of Israel from turning from God-approved sacrifices to sacrificing their own innocent children like the pagans around them. In Leviticus 18:21, God told the children of Israel: "And you shall not let any of your descendants pass through the fire to Molech, nor shall you profane the name of your God: I am the Lord." God went to great lengths to warn the Israelites against offering their children as sacrifices because it was well known that the nations around them took part in such infanticide. The question arises, "What in this world could convince a mother or father to offer their children to a god?" Let us investigate this matter further.

Wendy Davis writes for *Widdershins*—a self-proclaimed journal of unadulterated paganism. In an article on the World Wide Web, *As Old as the Moon: Sacrifice in History,* she stated: "The act of ritual murder is probably as old as we [humans—KB/EL] are. Throughout the ages, people sacrificed when they needed something. Our ancestors often **gave the best they had, their first-born**, to save themselves" (1995, emp. added). The most precious possession of a mother or father would be their first-born child. That child, however, would be not only precious, but also sinless. Sacrifice of anything less than that which is spotless and pure diminishes the inherent value of the sacrifice. Thus, it was believed that a sinless and pure sacrifice of such magnitude could wash away the sins of the parents (or, for that matter, the sins of an entire village!). Therefore, corrupt, perverse religions sprang up around the sacrifice of children, one of the most famous of which was that of Molech (see 2 Kings 23:10).

Yet even though the sacrifice of infants fulfilled the **sinless** aspect of a perfect sacrifice, it was lacking in other areas. For example, an "ordinary" infant born of peasant parents was not the most costly sacrifice available; a royal child of a king would be even better.

Thus, as Davis went on to observe, kings ultimately sacrificed their own children to appease "the gods."

But the sacrifice of a king's child still did not represent the perfect sacrifice, because the child did not go of his (or her) own free will. A free-will sacrifice of royal blood would come closest to the perfect offering. In an article titled *No Greater Sacrifice,* which appeared in *Widdershins,* one writer suggested: "Willing sacrifice is more interesting. Why does someone want to sacrifice himself or herself for what they believe in? Historically speaking, we must consider the sacred kings who sacrificed themselves for the Land" (see Andy, 1998). Yes, a king who offered himself of his own free will would be **almost** the perfect sacrifice. The only problem with such a concept was the fact that no king ever had lived a perfect life. As the *Widdershins* writer correctly observed, in an attempt to solve this, "[f]inally someone came up with the idea of one final sacrifice. One sacrifice to count for all the rest for all time. But who could be offered? It had to be someone very important; even kings were not good enough. Clearly, only a god was important enough to count as the last one" (Andy, 1998). Thus, it becomes clear why even the pagan world demanded a sacrifice that was sinless, royal, and higher in stature than other humans. Doane stated: "The belief of redemption from sin by the sufferings of a Divine Incarnation, whether by death on the cross or otherwise, was general and popular among the heathen, centuries before the time of Jesus of Nazareth" (1882, pp. 183-185).

Once we comprehend the need for the death of the savior-god, it is not difficult to see why humanity would want (and need) to see him defeat death. The writer of the book of Hebrews addressed this very point when he wrote that Christ allowed Himself to be sacrificed so that He "might deliver all them who through fear of death were all their lifetime subject to bondage" (2:15). Death holds more terror for man than perhaps anything else on Earth. It was for this reason that the Greeks invented Hercules—half man and half god—to conquer the Underworld, and the Egyptians formulated Osiris. Surely a savior-god who offered himself voluntarily as the sacrifice for all humanity could defeat mankind's dreaded enemy—Death. So, the idea of a sacrificial savior-god who victoriously defeats death through his resurrection came easily to the minds of people who knew that they needed forgiveness, and who desperately wanted to live past the grave.

And so, from a "universal frame of mind" different tribes and religions—spanning thousands of years—formulated their personal versions of what they thought a resurrected savior-god should be and do. Some said he was torn into fourteen pieces and scattered throughout the land of Egypt (e.g., Osiris). Others said he would look like a man but would possess superhuman physical strength and descend to the underworld to conquer Hades (e.g., Hercules). Yet one thing is certain: tales about a hero who saved mankind were on the lips of almost every storyteller. Trench stated correctly:

> No thoughtful student of the past records of mankind can refuse to acknowledge that through all its history there has run the hope of a redemption from the evil which oppresses it; and as little can deny that this hope has continually attached itself to some single man (n.d., p. 149).

But how can it be maintained, then, that the one savior for whom all humanity waited was, and is, Jesus?

JESUS—UNIQUE SAVIOR OF MANKIND

One important fact that cannot be ignored is that Jesus is the only **historical** figure Who fulfills the criteria necessary to justify, sanctify, and redeem mankind. No human's creative mind concocted the narrative of Jesus of Nazareth. Human eyes saw Him, and human ears heard Him. He walked and talked—lived and loved—on the streets of real cities and in the houses of real people. His life is the only life of any "savior-god" that can be (and has been) thoroughly documented. As Stephen Franklin remarked: "[T]he specific character of Biblical religion and, thus, of Christianity stems from the priority given to the historical-factual dimension of the Bible's basic teachings and doctrines" (1993, 17[1]:40).

Therefore, the story of Jesus Christ does not occupy a place amidst the pages of Greek mythology or ancient religious legend. But oh, how the skeptics wish that it did! As Freke and Gandy observed in *The Jesus Mysteries*:

> Early Literalist Christians mistakenly believed that the Jesus story was different from other stories of Osiris-Dionysus because Jesus alone had been a **historical** rather than a mythical figure. This has left Christians feeling that their faith is in opposition to all others, which it is not (1999, p. 13, emp. added).

Indeed, skeptics would delight in being able to place the story of Jesus on the same playing field as the stories of legendary savior-gods, because then the parallel stories could easily be relegated to myth, due to the fact that the stories cannot be verified historically. Trench wrote of such skeptics:

> Proving, as it is not hard to prove, those parallels to be groundless and mythical, to rest on no true historic basis, they hope that the great facts of the Christian's belief will be concluded to be as weak, will be involved in a common discredit (n.d., p. 135).

If infidels were able to create a straw man that could not stand up to the test of historical verifiability (like, for example, pagan legends and myths), and if they could place the story of Jesus in the same category as their tenuous straw man, then both supposedly would fall together. However, the story of Jesus of Nazareth refuses to fall. The stories of other savior-gods are admitted to be—even by those who invented them—nothing but fables (e.g., many of the Greeks realized that their fictitious stories were merely untrue legends that were totally unverifiable; see McCabe, 1926, p. 59). But the story of Jesus demands its rightful place in the annals of human history. Osiris, Krishna, Hercules, Dionysus, and the other mythological savior-gods stumble back into the shadows of fiction when compared to the documented life of Jesus of Nazareth. If the skeptic wishes to challenge the uniqueness of Jesus by comparing Him with other alleged savior-gods, he first must produce evidence that one of these savior-gods truly walked on the Earth, interacted with humanity, and impacted people's lives via both a sinless existence and incomparable teachings. Humanity always has desired a real-life savior-god; but can any of the alleged savior-gods that have been invented boast of a historical existence any more thoroughly documented than that of Christ? To ask is to answer

In addition, Jesus has a monopoly on being perfectly flawless. He lived life by the same moral rules that govern all humans, yet He never once made a mistake. The writer of Hebrews recorded: "For we have not a high priest that cannot be touched with the feeling of our infirmities; but one that hath been in all points tempted like as we are, **yet without sin**" (4:15, emp. added; cf. also 1 Peter 2:21-22). Renowned religious historian Philip Schaff wrote:

> In vain do we look through the entire biography of Jesus for a single stain or the slightest shadow of his moral character. There never lived a more harmless being on earth. He injured nobody, he took advantage of nobody. He never wrote an improper word. He never committed a wrong action (1913, pp. 32-33).

Bernard Ramm commented in a similar vein when he stated of Christ:

> There He stands, **sinless**. Whatever men may claim for being great, this is one thing they cannot. They may be brilliant or strong, fast or clever, creative or inspired, but not sinless. Sinless perfection and perfect sinlessness is what we would expect of God incarnate. The hypothesis and the facts concur (1953, p. 169, emp. in orig.).

Examine the stories of other savior-gods. See if they subjected themselves to the same rules as humans. See if they learned human nature and suffered unjustly, all the while never sinning with either their lips or their hearts. Try to find a savior like Christ who lived 30+ years on the Earth and yet never committed one shameful act. Norman Geisler summarized the situation as follows: "All men are sinners; God knows it and so do we. If a man lives an impeccable life and offers as the truth about himself that he is God incarnate we must take his claim seriously" (1976, p. 344). Jesus did "offer as the truth about himself that he is God incarnate." As John Stott noted:

> The most striking feature of the teaching of Jesus is that He was constantly talking about Himself.... This self-centeredness of the teaching of Jesus immediately sets Him apart from the other great religious teachers of the world. They were self-effacing. He was self-advancing. They pointed men away from themselves, saying, "That is the truth, so far as I perceive it; follow that." Jesus said, "I am the truth; follow me." The founders of the ethnic religions never dared say such a thing (1971, p. 23).

There is another important point to be considered, however. Who better to deny the idea that Jesus was perfect than those who spent the most time with Him? There is a grain of truth to the adage that "familiarity breeds contempt." Surely His closest friends would have observed some small demerit. Yet when we read the comments of His closest followers, we find that even they lauded Him as the only sinless man. The apostle Peter, who was rebuked publicly by Jesus, nevertheless called Him "a lamb without blemish and without spot" (1 Peter 1:19). One chapter later in the same epistle, Peter said that Jesus "did no sin, neither was guile found in his mouth" (2:22). Indeed, Christ even went so far as to invite anyone who dared, to convict Him of sin when He said: "Which of you convicts me of sin" (John 8:46). No one alive in His day could convict the Lord of sin; neither can anyone today. However, when one begins to examine the lives of the other alleged savior-gods, it soon becomes evident that these "heroes" committed fornication with humans, allowed their sinful tempers to flare, and raged with overt jealousy. Every supposed savior of mankind besides Jesus had an Achilles heel. If any such "savior" existed (other than Jesus) who did not have a vice or a sin, his life certainly cannot be documented historically. And if any savior-god besides Jesus could be documented historically, his life easily could be proven to be laden with sin.

Christ was Unique in His Teachings

Not only have the specific details of Christ's life come under allegations of plagiarism, but His teachings also have undergone intense scrutiny. Some have complained, for example, that Jesus' teachings were little more than warmed over Old Testament concepts. In the feature article he authored on Christ for the March 29, 1999 issue of *Newsweek* (the cover of which was titled "2000 Years of Jesus"), Kenneth Woodward suggested: "As scholars have long realized, there was little in the teachings of Jesus that cannot be found in the Hebrew Scriptures he expounded" (135[13]:54). The non-Christian Jew and the skeptic frequently view Jesus as an ancient teacher Who borrowed much of His material from the Hebrew text that had been in existence hundreds of years before He entered the global picture, since many of His sayings can be traced back centuries to the Jewish psalmist David, the prophet Isaiah, and a host of other ancient Hebrew writers. Others have complained that Christ's teachings had their origin in ancient pagan lore. Freke and Gandy suggested:

> ...[W]e discovered that even Jesus' teachings were not original, but had been anticipated by the Pagan sages.... Pagan critics of Christianity, such as the satirist Celsus, complained that this recent religion was nothing more than a pale reflection of their own ancient teachings (1999, pp. 5-6).

Thus, if it is to be argued successfully that Jesus truly is unique in His teachings, the incontrovertible fact that He used a considerable amount of ancient Hebrew literature must be explained, and certain important dissimilarities must be made manifest (between either Old Testament material or that from previous pagan sources). Otherwise, we have merely another Jewish rabbi who knew both heathen sources and the Scriptures well—just as a host of other Jewish rabbis did.

In order to explain why Jesus employed so much Hebrew literature, we must understand His relationship with that literature. A statement from Peter's first epistle is quite helpful in this regard:

> Of this salvation the prophets have inquired and searched carefully, who prophesied of the grace that would come to you, searching what, or what manner of time, the **Spirit of Christ** who was in them was indicating when He testified beforehand the sufferings of Christ and the glories that would follow (1 Peter 1:10-11, emp. added).

Peter's point of emphasis was that Christ was not just an interested **reader** of ancient Hebrew scripture; rather, He was its **Author**. He wrote the Jewish Old Testament through His Spirit that worked through the prophets. When He quoted Isaiah or Jeremiah, He neither copied their material nor plagiarized their truths. Quite the contrary, in fact. He simply quoted the texts that

He personally had inspired and published through the ancient holy men. As the famous "church father" Tertullian wrote in his *Apology*, "There is nothing so old as the truth" (chapter 47). To suggest that Christ's teachings were not unique because He quoted passages from the Old Testament would be like saying that the author of a particular book could not quote from that book in later lectures or publications, lest he be charged with plagiarism of his own material.

There are those, of course, who will discount the above argument by claiming that the New Testament has no authority to answer such questions. Thus, they will continue to claim that Jesus "borrowed" His ideas from the pages of Israel's texts. If they wish to defend such a viewpoint, then let them find in the Old Testament any description of eternal punishment comparable to the one Jesus provided in Mark 9:43. Where in the Old Testament Scriptures do we find that it is more difficult for a rich person to enter heaven than for a camel to go through the eye of a needle? Where in the Old Testament is the idea of loving one's neighbor developed to the extent that Christ described in the parable of the Good Samaritan? Jesus of Nazareth did not merely regurgitate Old Testament passages, adding jots and tittles as He went. Instead, He came to fulfill the Old Law, and to instigate a New Law with distinctive concepts and commands—a point the writer of Hebrews made quite clear when he stated: "In that he says, 'A new covenant,' he has made the first obsolete. Now what is becoming old is ready to vanish away" (8:13).

Even though it can be proven that Jesus did not plagiarize the Old Testament, the battle for the uniqueness of His teachings does not end there. Traces of concepts that predate Christ's earthly existence also can be found in His teachings. Earlier, we quoted from Augustine, who noted that Plato's followers claimed Christ had copied their philosophical hero (except, they opined, that Christ was not nearly as eloquent). Further, rabbi Hillel, who lived approximately fifty years before Jesus, taught: "What thou wouldest not have done to thee, do not that to others" (see Bales, n.d., p. 7). Confucius (and a host of other ancient writers) taught things that Jesus also taught. From China to Egypt, a steady stream of pagans uttered things that Christ, centuries later, likewise would say in one form or another. How, then, can the teachings of Christ be considered unique if they had been surfacing in different cultures and civilizations for hundreds of years before His visit to Earth? Perhaps this would be a good place to ask: What is the alternative? As Bales noted:

> If Christ had been **completely original**, He would have had to omit every truth which had been revealed in the Old Testament, or which had been discerned by the reason of man. If He had done this, His teaching would have been inadequate, for it would have omitted many moral and spiritual truths (n.d., p. 21, emp. added).

Jesus came not to reiterate ancient truths, but rather to synthesize those truths into a complete unit. He embodied every spiritual truth the world had ever seen or ever would see. As Bales commented: "Christ embodies all the moral good which is found in other religions, and He omits their errors" (p. 7). In his letter to the Christians in Colossae, Paul described Christ as the one "in whom are hidden **all the treasures of**

wisdom and knowledge" (2:3, emp. added). Christ's teachings are like gold; tiny amounts can be found in almost every area of the world–from ocean water to the human body. However, in order for that gold to be usable, it must be collected into a mass large enough to refine. Christ is the "refining pot" of all knowledge and wisdom, wherein the dross of error is purged from the precious metal of divine truth. While tiny specks of His teachings emerge from practically every religion, they can be refined only when collected as a whole in the essence of Jesus the Nazarene. Stephen Franklin put it like this:

> By providing echoes of Christian themes in every culture and in every religion, he [God—KB/EL] has given the entire human race some "handle" that allows them at least a preliminary understanding of the gospel when it is preached (1993, p. 51).

Furthermore, consider both the power and the authority evident in Christ's teachings. Even His enemies were unable to refute what He taught. When the Jewish Sanhedrin decided to take action against Him and dispatched its security force to seize Him, those officers returned empty handed and admitted: "No man **ever** spoke like this Man!" (John 7:46, emp. added). When He was only twelve years old and His parents accidentally left Him behind in Jerusalem, they returned to find Him in a discussion of religious matters with the learned scribes, "and all who heard Him were astonished at His understanding and answers" (Luke 2:47).

The Jews had long yearned for a Messiah ("Christ") Who would save and deliver them. The Samaritan woman Christ met at the well spoke of this very fact, to which He replied: "I who speak to you am He" (John 4:26). When Jesus was on trial before the Sanhedrin, Caiaphas the high priest demanded: "Tell us if you are the Christ, the Son of God?" His reply was firm: "It is as you said" (Matthew 26:63-64). He spoke with authority regarding the pre-human **past**, because He was there (John 1:1ff.). In the **present**, "there is no creature hidden from His sight, but all things are naked and open to the eyes of Him to whom we must give account" (Hebrews 4:13). And He knows the **future**, as is evident from even a cursory reading of His prophecies about the building of His church (Matthew 16:18), the sending of the Holy Spirit to the apostles (John 14:26), and His many descriptions of His ultimate return and the Day of Judgment (Matthew 25:31-46, et al.). All of this, and more, explains why Paul referred to Him as "King of kings, and Lord of lords" (1 Timothy 6:15). No one ever possessed, or spoke with, the kind of authority with which Christ was endowed, which is why He taught: "All authority has been given to Me in heaven and on earth" (Matthew 28:18). Fraudulent saviors never claimed such, nor had their own enemies confirmed such. Perhaps this is one reason why, in the feature article from *Time* magazine's December 6, 1999 cover story ("Jesus at 2000"), author Reynolds Price wrote:

> It would require much exotic calculation, however, to deny that the single most powerful figure—not merely in these two millennia but in all human history—has been Jesus of Nazareth.... [A] serious argument can be made that no one else's life has proved remotely as powerful and

> enduring as that of Jesus. It's an astonishing conclusion in light of the fact that Jesus was a man who lived a short life in a rural backwater of the Roman Empire [and] who died in agony as a convicted criminal... (154[23]:86).

Mythical saviors never had such an assessment made of their lives or more specifically of their teachings.

WHAT WOULD YOU EXPECT?

In his fascinating book, *What If Christ Had Never Been Born?*, D. James Kennedy discussed at length both the uniqueness of Jesus Christ and His singular impact on the Earth's inhabitants. In assessing that impact, Dr. Kennedy wrote:

> Jesus Christ has had an enormous impact—more than anybody else—on history. Had He never come, the hole would be a canyon about the size of a continent. Christ's influence on the world is immeasurable.... Whatever Jesus touched or whatever He did transformed that aspect of human life. Many people will read about the innumerable small incidents in the life of Christ while never dreaming that those casually mentioned "little" things were to transform the history of mankind (1994, p. 4).

Philip Schaff discussed Christ's influence when he wrote in his book, *The Person of Christ: The Miracle of History*:

> This Jesus of Nazareth, without money or arms, conquered more millions than Alexander, Caesar, Mohammed, and Napoleon; without science and learning, He shed more light on things human and divine than all philosophers and scholars combined; without the eloquence of schools, He

> spoke such words of life as were never spoken before or since, and produced effects which lie beyond the reach of orator or poet; without writing a single line, He set more pens in motion, and furnished themes for more sermons, orations, discussions, learned volumes, works of art, and songs of praise, than the whole army of great men of ancient and modern times (1913, p. 33).

The simple fact is, Jehovah left no stone unturned in preparing the world for the coming of the One Who would save mankind. Through a variety of avenues, He alerted the inhabitants of planet Earth regarding the singular nature of the One Who was yet to come, as well as the importance of believing in and obeying Him. Humanity's sins can be forgiven only by a sinless Savior. A mythological sacrifice can forgive only mythological sins, but Jesus truly is the Lamb of God "who takes away the sin of the world" (John 1:29). As Norman Geisler put it:

> It is one thing to claim deity and quite another to have the credentials to support that claim. Christ did both. He offered three unique and miraculous facts as evidence of his claim: the fulfillment of prophecy, a uniquely miraculous life, and the resurrection from the dead. All of these are historically provable and unique to Jesus of Nazareth. We argue, therefore, that Jesus alone claims to be and proves to be God (1976, p. 339).

CHAPTER 4

THE PREDICTED MESSIAH

In hindsight, a good mystery fits together perfectly, like the various pieces of an intricate puzzle that need but one final piece to link the parts that form the completed magnificent panorama. Until that final piece is added, the mystery is virtually impossible to grasp in its entirety. In fact, while the mystery is developing, the inquisitor's greatest challenge is to assess correctly which pieces of information or evidence are of significance and which are the banal elements that add nothing of consequence to the story. Is it important that Mr. Brown forgot his hat at the train station? Does it matter that the water faucet in the kitchen suddenly is not working properly? Inevitably, the astute inquisitor accurately pinpoints those elements in the story that are of great import. The less astute inaccurately labels ordinary events as important, or fails to understand fully events that were of major consequence.

Such is the case when approaching the study of the predicted Messiah, or, as it were, when solving the mystery of the Messiah. Anyone familiar with New Testament writings is quite familiar with the term "mystery" as it is applied to God's plan for the redemption of the human race through the predicted Messiah. Paul wrote concerning this mystery: "But we speak the wisdom of God in a mystery, the hidden wisdom which God ordained before ages for our glory" (1 Corinthians 2:7). In his letter to the Colossians, he stated: "I became a minister according to the stewardship from God which was given to me for you, to fulfill the word of God, the mystery which has been hidden from ages and from generations, but now has been revealed to his saints" (1:25-26). Paul's epistle to the Ephesians contains similar comments: "[I]f indeed you have heard of the dispensation of the grace of God which was given to me for you, how that by revelation He made known to me the mystery...which in other ages was not made known to the sons of men as it has now been revealed by the Spirit to His holy apostles and prophets" (3:2-3,5).

The New Testament writers identified for us several characteristics of this Messianic mystery: (1) The mystery revolves around the prophesied Messiah and the redemption of mankind; (2) The mystery is one that has been hidden in various ways from all generations of people prior to the time of the New Testament; (3) The various tenets of the mystery are divinely revealed and made known only through divine communication; (4) During the times of the New Testament writers, God revealed the final piece of the mystery to the New Testament writers themselves.

The intention of this discussion is to trace out the various divinely revealed tenets of the Messianic mystery. Upon completion of that task, we must then determine if, in truth, the New Testament writers did possess the final, completing piece of that mystery. We dealt in the previous chapter with the traces of a Savior originating from various sources outside the biblical writings. Therefore, since the Hebrew Scriptures are renowned for being the most complete repository of Messianic predictions available, we will focus our attention upon them.

OLD TESTAMENT SCRIPTURES

In contemplating the Old Testament, Jewish Scriptures, it would be beneficial for us to consider several important features of the writings. First, the opening eleven chapters of the first book, Genesis, do not relate to the Hebrews only, but to the broader scope of humanity as a whole. These chapters describe the creation of the Universe, the fall of man from his perfect state of innocence, the wickedness of man and the destructive, world-wide Flood, and the repopulation of the Earth. They contain approximately 2,000 years of history, not a year of which necessarily has anything to do with the Jewish nation, any more than with any other nation.

Second, the remainder of the Old Testament, from Genesis 12-Malachi, focuses primarily on the descendants of Abraham. Note that the narratives and terms often used to describe these descendants are none too flattering. They are called stubborn, stiff-necked, sinful, rebellious, and a host of adjectives equally as caustic (see Deuteronomy 9:7; Ezekiel 2:3-10; Hosea 4:16). And yet, these descendants of Abraham are the ones responsible for preserving the very Scriptures that repeatedly rebuked them for their idolatrous backsliding from God. Remember, too, that they could have altered and preserved these writings in a more flattering form. From archaeological finds we have learned that other nations surrounding ancient Israel often chose to embellish their history, intentionally excluding derogatory remarks or events concerning themselves.

Why did the Israelites preserve the writings as they did? The answer to this is actually twofold. First, they believed the particular writings that they preserved to be inspired by God, a belief that can be proven beyond doubt (see Thompson, 2001). But second, each of the 39 books contains a calculated revelation describing some aspect of the coming Messiah, who, according to these Scriptures, is not only destined to save the nation of Israel, but the entire world. In fact, the reader cannot progress far into the Old Testament writings before he is inundated with descriptions of, and predictions concerning, the coming Messiah.

WERE THE JEWS LOOKING FOR A MESSIAH?

It has been suggested that the ancient Jewish scribes, rabbis, and general population were not really looking for a personal Messiah. Eminently respected Messianic Jewish author David Baron first published his work, *Rays of Messiah's Glory*, in 1886. In that volume, Baron wrote:

> I am aware also that in recent times many intelligent Jews, backed by rationalistic, so-called Christians...deny that there is hope of a Messiah in the Old Testament Scriptures, and assert that the prophecies on which Christians ground such a belief contain only "vague anticipations and general hopes, but no definite predictions of a personal Messiah," and that consequently the alleged agreement of the gospel history with prophecy is imaginary (2000, p. 16).

In his statements that refute the "non-Messianic" view of Old Testament Scripture, Baron wrote: "Even Maimonides, the great antagonist of Christianity, composed that article of the Jewish creed which unto the present day is repeated daily by every true Jew: 'I believe with a perfect faith that the Messiah will come, and although His coming be delayed, I will await His daily appearance' " (p. 18). He commented further: "Aben Ezra, Rashi, Kimchi, Abarbanel, and almost every other respectable and authoritative Jewish commentator, although not recognizing Jesus as the Messiah, are yet unanimous that a personal Messiah is taught in the Old Testament Scriptures" (pp. 19-20). Baron also noted that only an "insignificant minority of the Jews" had dared to suggest that the Old Testament lacks definitive predictions of a personal Messiah. He then eloquently stated: "[W]ith joy we behold the nation [Jews—KB/EL], as such, still clinging to the anchor which has been the mainstay of their national existence for so many ages—the hope of a personal Messiah, which is the essence of the Old Testament Scriptures" (p. 20).

In his volume, *The Messiah in the Old Testament: In Light of Rabbinical Writings*, Risto Santala wrote: "If we study the Bible and the Rabbinic literature carefully, we cannot fail to be surprised at the abundance of Messianic interpretation in the earliest works known to us.... [T]he Talmud states unequivocally: 'All the prophets prophesied only for the days of the Messiah' " (1992, p. 22).

In regard to specific Old Testament prophecies, a plethora of rabbinical commentary verifies that the nation of Israel certainly had in view a coming Messiah. Concerning Genesis 49:10, the noted author Aaron Kligerman wrote: "The rabbis of old, though not agreeing with each other as to the meaning of the root Shiloh, were almost unanimous in applying the term to the Messiah" (1957, pp. 19-20). Immediately after this statement, Kligerman listed the Targum Onkelos, Targum Jerusalem, and the Peshito all as referring to Genesis 49:10 as a Messianic prophecy pointing toward an individual, personal Messiah (p. 20). With reference to Genesis 49:10, David Baron wrote:

> With regard to this prophecy, the first thing I want to point out is that **all antiquity agrees in interpreting it of a personal Messiah**. This is the view of the LXX Version [Septuagint—KB/EL]; the Targumim of Onkelos, Yonathan, and Jerusalem; the Talmud; the Sohar; the ancient book of "Bereshith Rabba;" and among modern Jewish commentators, even Rashi, who says, "Until Shiloh come, that is King Messiah, Whose is the kingdom" (2000, p. 258, emp. added).

Concerning the book of Isaiah and the predictive, Messianic prophecy contained within it, Santala stated: "The Messianic nature of the book of Isaiah is so clear that the oldest Jewish sources, the Targum, Midrash and Talmud, speak of the Messiah in connection with 62 separate verses" (1992, pp. 164-165). Santala then, in a footnote, proceeded to list several of those verses, including Isaiah 4:2, 9:5, 10:27, 11:1, 11:6, 14:29, 16:1, 28:5, 42:1, 43:10, 52:13, and 60:1 (p. 165).

The prophet Jeremiah contains material that has long been recognized as Messianic in nature. Concerning Jeremiah 23:5-6, David Baron wrote: "There is scarcely any contrary opinion among ancient and modern Jews but that this is a Messianic prophecy" (2000, p. 78).

In truth, statements that verify that the ancient Israelite nation recognized certain passages in the Old Testament as Messianic are legion. Regardless of what a person believes about the identity of the Messiah, it cannot be gainsaid that the nation of Israel, through the influence of the Old Testament writers, has been waiting for His coming.

THE PROTEVANGELIUM

Virtually from the first glimpse of human life on the Earth, traces of the predicted Messiah were divinely revealed to mankind. All too familiar is the tragic story of the fall of man. Under God's gracious care, Adam and Eve were specially designed to suit each other's needs and were ushered into the Edenic Paradise, the joys of which humanity has not seen since nor will see again this side of eternity. God gave the first family only one prohibitory commandment—that they should not eat from the tree of the knowledge of good and evil. If they chose to rebel against this lone prohibition, God informed them that the consequence would be death. Yet despite God's gracious warning, Eve's senses were dulled by her evil desires, and she soon fell prey to the deceitfulness of sin, convincing her husband Adam to join in her rebellion.

Into this scene of shame and sin, God brought judgment upon all parties involved. Death would be the consequence of this sinful action, as well as increased pain in childbirth for the woman and increased hardship and toil for the man. Yet in the midst of God's curse upon the serpent, He included a ray of glorious hope for humanity. To the serpent he said: "And I will put enmity between your seed and her Seed; He shall bruise your head, and you shall bruise His heel" (Genesis 3:15). This brief statement made by God to the serpent concerning the Seed of woman is often referred to as the protevangelium. J.A. Huffman commented on the passage:

> Here the prophecy of a deliverer is unmistakably uttered. Even a temporary bruise, that of the heel, suggesting the apparent, momentary defeat of the deliverer is predicted: but, at the same time, the deliverer's ultimate and final triumph is prophesied, in his bruising of the serpent's head, which means a fatal blow (1956, p. 38).

The Jewish scholar, Aaron Kligerman, noted that three things stand out in this first prediction of the Messiah, "namely that the Deliverer must be—(A) of the *seed of woman* and (B) That He is to be *temporarily hindered* and (C) *Finally victorious* (1957, p. 13, italics in orig.). Kligerman further noted that the ancient rabbinical opinions found in the Palestinian Targum testify "that in Genesis 3:15 there is promised a healing of the bite in the heel from the serpent, which is to take place 'at the end of the days, in the days of King Messiah' " (p. 14). [NOTE: The Targums "are interpretive renderings of the books of Hebrew Scriptures...into Aramaic" (Metzger, 1993). Such versions were needed when the major populations of the Jews no longer spoke Hebrew as their primary language. Metzger further explains that the oral Targum began as a simple paraphrase of the text, "but eventually it became more elaborate and incorporated explanatory details." John Stenning, in his detailed article on the Targum, explained that oral Targum was introduced several years prior to the first century A.D. in connection with "the custom of reading sections from the Law at the weekly services in the synagogues" (1911).]

Of the protevangelium, Charles A. Briggs, in his classic work *Messianic Prophecy*, noted:

> Thus we have in this fundamental prophecy explicitly a struggling, suffering, but finally victorious human race, and implicitly a struggling, suffering and finally victorious son of woman, a second Adam, the head of the race.... The protevangelium is a faithful miniature of the entire history of humanity, a struggling seed ever battling for ultimate victory.... [u]ntil it is realized in the sublime victories of redemption" (1988, p. 77).

Briggs went on to comment that the protevangelium "is the only Messianic prophecy which has been preserved from the revelations made by God to the antediluvian world" (p. 77).

Here, then, is the seminal prophecy made to pave the way for all others that would deal with the coming of the great Deliverer of mankind. Several qualities of this coming Deliverer are readily apparent. First, He will come in human form as the seed of woman. Second, He will defeat the effects of sin brought about by the fall of man and the entrance of sin into the world. Third, He will be hindered in His redemptive activity by the serpent, Satan, who will inflict upon Him a minor wound. Fourth, He will ultimately overcome the wound of Satan and finally triumph. In this first prediction of the Messiah, we catch an underlying theme of a suffering, victorious redeemer—a theme that will be fleshed out in the remaining pages of the Old Testament.

THE SEED OF ABRAHAM

The protevangelium in Genesis 3:15 predicted that the conquering Messiah would belong to the seed of woman, taking on a human form. But that feature alone, admittedly, does not help much in identifying the Messiah, since billions of people have been born of woman. In order for Messianic prophecy to prepare its readers for the actual Messiah, the scope would need to be narrowed.

Such narrowing of the Messianic scope can be seen in God's promise to the patriarch, Abraham. In Genesis 12, the Bible records the fact that God specifically chose Abraham from among all the peoples of the world (Genesis 12:1-3). Through Abraham, God promised that all the nations of the world would be blessed, and that Abraham's descendants would multiply as the sand of the sea and the stars of the sky. As Huffman noted, "It was to Abraham, the son of Terah, a descendant of Shem, that God gave a peculiar promise, one which could not be omitted in any serious effort to trace the Messianic hope" (1956, p. 41). For many years, this promise of progeny remained unfulfilled due to the fact that Abraham's wife, Sarah, was barren. In order to "help" God fulfill His promise, Abraham and Sarah devised a plan by which Abraham could have a child. Sarah sent her handmaid, Hagar, to serve as a surrogate wife to Abraham. As a result of this union, Hagar conceived and gave birth to a child named Ishmael.

In Genesis 17, God renewed His covenant with Abraham and instructed Abraham to institute circumcision as a sign of the covenant. In Genesis 17:19, God informed Abraham that Sarah would have a son named Isaac. In an interesting conversation with God, Abraham petitioned God to let Ishmael be the son of promise and the heir of the covenant that God made. Yet God insisted that Ishmael was not the son of promise and that the promise of all nations being blessed through Abraham's descendants would not pass through Ishmael, but would be fulfilled only through Isaac. God said: "But My covenant I will establish with Isaac, whom Sarah shall bear to you at this set time next year" (Genesis 17:21). James Smith, in writing about God's promise to bless all nations through Abraham, noted that this promise "has Messianic implications. Both the Church Fathers and Jewish Rabbis so interpreted it" (1993, p. 47). Aaron Kligerman concurred when he wrote about God's promise to Abraham: "This is more than the promise of 'The Hope of a Prosperous Era.' It is a promise of the coming of a 'Personal Messiah' " (1957, pp. 17-18). At this point in human history, then, the Messianic implications fall to the descendants of Isaac. It is important not to miss the significance of the Messianic hope through Abraham and Isaac. The scope of the Messiah has been narrowed from all other peoples and nations of the world, to a single nomadic family. And yet, not just to Abraham's family in its entirety, but to only one of Abraham's sons—Isaac.

But the picture becomes even clearer with the birth of the twin sons of Isaac and Rebekah. Because of abnormalities with her pregnancy, Rebekah went to inquire of the Lord about her situation. To answer her questions, the Lord said: "Two nations are in your womb, two peoples shall be separated from your body; one people shall be stronger than the other, and the older shall serve the younger" (Genesis 25:23). Concerning this passage, Briggs noted: "This prediction breaks up the seed of Isaac into two nations, assigns the headship with the blessing to Jacob, and makes Edom subject to him" (1988, p. 90). The fact that the promised Messiah would come through Jacob's descendants becomes increasingly clear throughout the Genesis narrative that tells the stories of Jacob and Esau. God confirmed the promise to Jacob in Genesis 28:14, when He said to the patriarch: "Also your descendants shall be as the dust of the earth; you shall spread abroad to the west and the east, to the north and the south; and **in you and in your seed all the families of the earth shall be blessed**" (emp. added). The picture of the Messiah continues to become increasingly focused: The seed of woman, the seed of Abraham, the seed of Isaac, the seed of Jacob.

TWO MESSIAHS: A SUFFERING SERVANT AND REIGNING KING

Throughout the Old Testament, various Messianic passages refer to a majestic, glorious King who will reign over a never-ending kingdom. Yet, at the same time, other Messianic prophecies depict a suffering Messiah who will bear the guilt and sin of the entire world. Because these two aspects of Messianic prophecy seem contradictory, many in the ancient Jewish community could not understand how such diverse prophetic sentiments could be fulfilled in a single individual. Due to this conundrum, ancient and modern Jews have posited the idea that two Messiahs would come: one would be the suffering Servant, while the other would be the glorious King.

Concerning this separation of the Messiah into two different individuals, John Ankerberg and his colleagues John Weldon and Walter Kaiser wrote:

> [T]hey (early Jewish rabbis—KB/EL) could not reconcile the statements that so clearly spoke of a suffering and dying Messiah with those verses in other passages that spoke of a triumphant and victorious Messiah. What is important to note is that they did recognize that both pictures somehow applied to the Messiah. But they assumed it was impossible to reconcile both views in one person. Rather than seeing one Messiah in two different roles, they saw two Messiahs—the suffering and dying Messiah, called "Messiah ben Joseph," and the victorious conquering Messiah, called "Messiah ben David" (1989, pp. 57-58).

Jewish rabbi Robert M. Cohen stated:

> The rabbis saw that scripture portrayed two different pictures of King Messiah. One would conquer and reign and bring Israel back to the land by world peace and bring the fullness of obedience to the Torah. They called him Messiah ben David. The other picture is of a servant who would die and bear Israel's sin that they refer to as the "leprous one" based on Isaiah 53 (Cohen, n.d.; also see Parsons, 2003-2006).

It is evident, from the rabbinical view of two Messiahs, that the themes of suffering and regal authority were so vividly portrayed in Old Testament Messianic prophecy that both themes demanded fulfillment. To suggest two Messiah's provided such a fulfillment. However, the dual Messianic idea failed to comprehend the actual nature of Messianic prophecy, and missed a primary facet of the Messianic personality: that the Messiah would be **both** a suffering Servant and a majestic King. As Huffman rightly observed: "The theme of Messianism is composed of two inseparable strands or threads—the scarlet and the golden, or the suffering and the reigning, or the priestly and the royal" (1956, p. 7). To misunderstand or miss either of these two interwoven threads would be to miss the Messiah completely.

Genesis 49:10—Shiloh

The Lord kept His promise to Jacob and multiplied his descendants exceedingly. His twelve sons and their wives and children escorted him to Egypt to live in the land of Goshen at the behest of Joseph, who had been elevated in Egypt as the Pharaoh's chief advisor. As Jacob neared the end of his rather long life (over 130 years, Genesis 47:9), he gathered his sons around his death bed, and stated: "Gather together, that I may tell you what shall befall you in the last days" (Genesis 49:1). Following this introductory statement, Jacob proceeded to address each of his sons and bestow blessings (or in some cases, curses) on his descendants.

In the midst of his final speech, in his blessing on Judah, Jacob stated: "The scepter shall not depart from Judah, nor a lawgiver from between his feet, until Shiloh comes; and to Him shall be the obedience of the people" (Genesis 49:10). The Messianic nature of this statement has long been recognized and discussed in ancient Jewish circles. As previously stated, David Baron wrote: "With regard to this prophecy, the first thing I want to point out is that **all antiquity agrees in interpreting it of a personal Messiah**. This is the view of the LXX. Version; the Targumim of Onkelos, Yonathan, and Jerusalem; the Talmud; the Sohar; the ancient book of 'Bereshith Rabba;' and among modern Jewish commentators, even Rashi, who says, 'Until Shiloh come, that is King Messiah, Whose is the kingdom'" (2000, p. 258, emp. added). Aaron Kligerman added: "The rabbis of old, though not agreeing with each other as to the meaning of the root Shiloh, were almost unanimous in applying the term to the Messiah" (1957, p. 19-20). Santala, in his discussion of several of the oldest Jewish documents available, wrote:

> Targum Onqulos says of Judah's scepter that it will not depart "*until the Messiah comes, he who has the power to reign.*" Targum Jonathan puts it that the verse refers to "*the age of the Messiah-King, the King who will come as the youngest of his children.*" Targum Yerushalmi speaks of the 'time' when "*the Messiah-King will come*" (1992, p. 50, italics in orig.).

Much commentary and debate surrounds the "Shiloh" prophecy found in Genesis 49:10. It is often viewed as an indication of the time that the Messiah should arrive on the scene. As can be deduced from Kligerman's quote, the actual origin and exact meaning of the word Shiloh are disputed in many scholarly circles. Yet, despite the controversy in reference to this prophecy, the one aspect of it that stands out is the central idea that this is a Messianic prophecy. As such, it narrows the identity of the Messiah even further to a descendant, not just of Abraham, Isaac, and Jacob, but to the house of Judah.

The Son of David

Of all the monarchs that possessed the throne of Israel, none is as storied as King David. From his youth he proved himself to be a courageous, valiant warrior who trusted in the Lord. He was described as a man after God's own heart (1 Samuel 13:14). He wrote many of the Psalms, and ushered in a united kingdom that paved the way for the majestic reign of his son, Solomon.

David's relationship to the Messiah is a rather interesting one. First, Jewish antiquity recognized the fact that the Messiah would be the Son of David. Santala commented: "*Tradition ascribes 73 of the 150 psalms to King David.* In the Rabbinic literature the Messiah is constantly referred to as the 'Son of David.' For this reason, everywhere the future blessing of the house of David is described, the Sages saw Messianic material" (1992, p. 109, italics in orig.).

Such Messianic sentiments in regard to David find their seminal origin in the promise made by God to David through the prophet Nathan. In 2 Samuel 7, the text narrates the events that lead to this promise. David had become a great king and his reign had spread far and wide. Due to his love for the Lord, he wanted to show honor to God by building a glorious temple in which the Ark of the Covenant could be housed. He mentioned his idea to the prophet Nathan, who immediately encouraged the building plans. But soon after Nathan had told David to do all that was in his heart, God conveyed to Nathan that He did not want David to build a temple. Instead, God would commission David's son, Solomon, to construct the magnificent edifice. Yet, in God's message to David, He promised: "And your house and your kingdom shall be established forever before you. Your throne shall be established forever" (2 Samuel 7:16).

In later Psalms, the promise of David's descendant reigning over an eternal Kingdom is expanded and given more substance. Psalm 89 contains several Messianic aspects, not the least of which is the following statement: "I have made a covenant with My chosen, I have sworn to My Servant David: 'Your seed I will establish forever, and build up your throne to all generations' " (vss. 3-4). Psalm 132 contains a very similar statement: "The Lord has sworn in truth to David; He will not turn from it: 'I will set upon your throne the fruit of your body. If your sons will keep My covenant and My testimony which I shall teach them, their sons also shall sit upon your throne forevermore."

Along with the various inspired psalmists, other Old Testament writers noted the Messianic lineage through David and his throne. One of the most memorable of all Messianic predictions from the Old Testament, Isaiah 9:6-7, mentioned the Messianic reign upon the throne of David:

> For unto us a Child is born, unto us a Son is given; and the government will be upon His shoulder. And His name will be called Wonderful, Counselor, Mighty God, Everlasting Father, Prince of Peace. Of the increase of His government and peace there will be no end, upon the throne of David and over His kingdom, to order it and establish it with judgment and justice from that time forward, even forever. The zeal of the Lord of hosts will perform this.

Yet, along with the fact that the Messiah was to be of the seed of David and reign on His throne, at least one Psalm places David in a subservient position to this majestic Messianic ruler. Psalm 110 opens with the statement: "The Lord said to my Lord, 'Sit at My right hand, till I make Your enemies Your footstool' " (Psalm 110:1). In regard to Psalm 110, Briggs noted: "The 110th Psalm is in the form of an utterance from Jahveh respecting the son of David. It is therefore a prediction that unfolds the prediction of Nathan" (1988, p. 132). Walter Kaiser, in his discussion of Psalm 110, wrote: "While the external evidence that this psalm is Messianic is large, the internal evidence is just as overwhelming" (1995, p. 94). In reference to the Messiah mentioned in the first verse, Kaiser stated: "That unnamed Lord is a royal person, for he was invited to 'sit at [God the Father's] right hand....' If the God of the universe invited this other Sovereign to take such a distinguished seat alongside himself, then we may be sure he was no one less than the promised Messiah, invited to participate in the divine government of the world" (p. 94).

Psalm 110 adds an interesting aspect to the character and position of the Messiah. Not only would the Messiah be born from the seed of David and reign on the throne of David, He also would be exalted to a position far above David, to such an extent that David called him "Lord" in Psalm 110. David's statements in this Psalm not only speak to the pre-existence of the Messiah before David, but also to the pre-eminence that the Messiah would assume.

With these details, the portrait of the Messiah becomes increasingly sharp. He was to come from the seed of woman and crush the power of Satan. He was to be of the seed of Abraham, Isaac, Jacob, Judah and now David. He would rule on the throne of David, yet He existed before David and was so preeminent that David called Him Lord. And there would be no end to His glorious, majestic kingdom.

THE SUFFERING SERVANT

Anyone who reads the Old Testament would be hard pressed to miss the idea of the Messiah's glorious regal prominence. Yet, as equally transparent is the idea that the Messiah was to suffer. The protevangelium in Genesis 3:15 makes reference to this suffering in the statement about the heel of the Seed of woman being bruised, but it does not include the details of this suffering. The theme of suffering introduced in Genesis 3:15 is expanded in the remainder of the Old Testament.

Isaiah 52:13-53:12

The passage of Scripture found in Isaiah 52:13-53:12 stands as a somber reminder of the horrendous suffering that the Messiah would endure. The text mentions that He would be highly exalted and extolled (52:13). And yet His appearance would be marred more than any man (52:14). He would not be physically attractive (53:2), and He would be despised and rejected by men, familiar with sorrows and grief (53:4). He would be perfect and without sin (53:9), and yet He would be beaten, suffer, and die for the sins of the Lord's people (53:5-6,11). This suffering Servant would be killed among the wicked, but buried among the rich (53:8-9). Yet, in spite of His death (or even because of it), He would be numbered among the great and divide the spoil with the strong (53:12).

Needless to say, this picture of the Messiah seems to stand in stark contrast to the glorious King on David's throne. As has been mentioned, this contrast has caused some to concoct two Messiahs to accommodate the prophecies. Still others have attempted to discount Messianic prophecies such as Isaiah 52:13-53:12. Some have suggested that this passage of Scripture is not Messianic in nature, but that the servant under discussion represents the collective nation of Israel. Along these lines, David Baron noted: "Modern Jews, in common with a number of rationalistic so-called Christians, are trying hard these days to weaken the Messianic application of this remarkable prophecy" (2000, p. 225). James Smith stated:

> The Messianic interpretation of Isaiah 53 was acknowledged by Jewish authorities until the Middle Ages. Almost all Christian leaders until the beginning of the nineteenth century saw in this passage a clear picture of the suffering, death and resurrection of the Messiah. Jews and some Christian scholars now hold primarily to the collective view of the Servant: The Servant is Israel as a whole, or the remnant. The traditional view, however, has much to commend it (1993, p. 307).

That the ancient Jewish community, and the bulk of scholars for the last 2,000 years, have recognized Isaiah 53 as a prophecy concerning a personal, individual Messiah cannot be questioned. Baron correctly commented regarding this sentiment: "That until recent times this prophecy has been almost universally received by Jews as referring to Messiah is evident from

Targum Yonathan, who introduces Messiah by name in chapter lii 13, from the Talmud ("Sanhedrin," fol. 98, b); and from Zohar, a book which the Jews as a rule do not mention without the epithet 'holy...' " (2000, p. 226).

The recent view that Isaiah 53 refers to the nation of Israel not only garners little (if any) support from ancient Jewish commentators, it collapses under the scrutiny of critical examination. The foremost objection to the view that Israel collectively is the Servant in Isaiah 53 is the fact that the Servant is described as perfect and sinless (53:9), not deserving the punishment that He willingly accepts for the sins of God's people. No one remotely familiar with the nation of Israel as portrayed in the Old Testament would dare suggest that they were sinless. From their first few steps out of Egypt and into freedom they began to provoke God and bring judgment upon themselves. On numerous occasions the Old Testament depicts the Israelites' sin of such a rebellious nature that God executed thousands of them. One fundamental aspect of an atoning sacrifice in Old Testament literature was its condition of spotless perfection. No nation of mere mortal men, including the ancient Israelite nation, could suffice as an atoning sacrifice for sins, as the Servant does in Isaiah 53. Nor could a sinful nation make another group of people "righteous" as the Lord's Servant would. Furthermore, the Servant of the Lord is depicted as being stricken for "transgressions of my people." If the Servant was collectively depicted as the nation of Israel, then who would be the Lord's people in 53:8? [NOTE: For a more complete refutation of Israel as the Servant of the Lord in Isaiah 53, see Baron, 2000, pp. 225-251.]

Indeed, the evidence points overwhelmingly to the fact that Isaiah 53 stands as one of the most poignant portrayals in all of the Old Testament of an individual, suffering Messiah. As Smith correctly noted: "The Servant of the Lord here is portrayed in a strongly individualistic way. It takes rich imagination or strong prejudice to see the Servant here as a symbol for Israel, the remnant, the prophets, or any other group" (p. 1993, p. 307). Kaiser similarly commented: "Undoubtedly, this is the summit of OT prophetic literature. Few passages can rival it for clarity on the suffering, death, burial, and resurrection of the Messiah (1995, p. 178).

VARIOUS SPECIFIC MESSIANIC PROPHECIES

In addition to the broad strokes portraying the Messiah as a reigning king and suffering servant, there are a host of more specific, detailed prophecies that relate to His coming. In regard to the number of Messianic prophecies, Santala wrote: "It is estimated that the Old Testament contains altogether some 456 prophecies concerning Christ. Of these 75 are to be found in the Pentateuch, 243 in the Prophets and 138 in the 'Writings' and Psalms" (1992, p. 149; cf. Free and Vos, 1992, p. 241).

Space prohibits a listing of all of these prophecies, but a representative sampling is appropriate. The Messiah was to be born in Bethlehem in Judea (Micah 5:2) of a virgin (Isaiah 7:14). He was to be betrayed by a friend (Psalm 41:9) for thirty pieces of silver (Zechariah 11:13). The Lord's Ruler would come into Jerusalem riding on the foal of a donkey (Zechariah 9:9). He would be buried with the rich (Isaiah 53:9). During His suffering, His clothes would be distributed to those who cast lots for them (Psalm 22:18). His attackers would pierce Him (Zechariah 12:10). Even though His physical suffering would be severe, His bones would not be broken (Psalm 34:20). And in spite of His death, His physical body would not experience decay (Psalm 16:10). This small sampling of specific prophetic details is only a fraction of the many Old Testament prophecies that exist. The prophecies were specifically designed to be an efficient mechanism by which the Jewish community could recognize the Messiah when He arrived.

WHO IS THE MESSIAH?

When all of the pieces of the Messianic puzzle are put together, one individual stands out as the only person who fulfilled every single prophecy in minute detail—Jesus Christ. The life and activities of Jesus Christ as recorded in the New Testament documents blend the theme of a regal monarch and a suffering servant into one magnificent portrait of the triumphant Jesus who was the sacrificial lamb at His death on the cross, and Who became the triumphant Lion of Judah in His resurrection from the grave. The lineage of Jesus Christ is meticulously traced in order to show that He qualified as the Seed of Abraham, of Isaac, of Jacob, of Judah, and of David (see Matthew 1 and Luke 3:23-38). The narrative detailing His birth verifies that He was born in Bethlehem of Judea, from which city the Messiah would arise (Luke 2:1-7). The birth narrative also intricately portrays the pre-existence of Jesus before time began, fulfilling the prophecy that the Messiah would come before King David. Furthermore, Jesus did, in fact, enter Jerusalem riding on the foal of a donkey (Matthew 21:1-11).

The New Testament narratives depicting the death of Jesus Christ verify that Jesus was betrayed by His friend and sold for exactly 30 pieces of silver (Matthew 24:14-16). At His death His bones were not broken, soldiers cast lots for His garments, and His side was pierced with a spear (John 19:33-37 and Matthew 27:35). During His suffering, He was numbered with the transgressors as Isaiah 53 predicted by being crucified between two thieves, and at His death He was buried in the tomb of a wealthy man as was also foretold (Matthew 27:57). This type of verification could continue for many pages. The life of Jesus Christ of Nazareth, as depicted in the New Testament documents, was designed to fulfill the Messianic prophecy of the Old Testament.

Due to this overwhelming congruence of the life of Jesus Christ with the predictive Messianic prophecy of the Old Testament, some have suggested that Jesus was an imposter who was able, by masterful manipulation, to so artificially organize His life as to make it look like He was the Messiah. Such a contention cannot be reasonably maintained in light of the fact that many of the prophecies were far beyond His control. Obviously, it would be impossible for a person to arrange where he would be born. Furthermore, it would be impossible to coordinate events so that He could make sure that He was buried in the tomb of a rich man or crucified among thieves. How could the betrayal price of Judas be manipulated by Jesus? And how, pray tell, would Jesus have managed to arrange it so that soldiers cast lots for His clothing? The idea that Jesus manipulated events to make it appear as if He was the Messiah not only is indefensible, but it also speaks to the fact that Jesus obviously was the fulfillment of the Old Testament, Messianic prophecies.

Others have objected to Jesus as the Messiah based on the idea that the New Testament documents are not reliable, and were artificially concocted to describe things that Jesus never really did. This objection also falls flat in light of the actual evidence. It cannot be denied that the New Testament has proven itself to be the most reliable book in ancient history. When it records people, places, and events that are checkable using archaeological means, those people, places, and events invariably prove to be factual and historic (see chapter two). Again, the abundant evidence verifies that the New Testament is accurate and factual. Many of the Messianic prophecies documented in the New Testament do not describe anything inherently miraculous. There was nothing miraculous about Jesus being buried in a rich man's tomb. Nor was there anything miraculous about Jesus riding into Jerusalem on the foal of a donkey, or being betrayed by His friend for 30 pieces of silver. These events are, if not ordinary, at least very plausible, everyday events that theoretically could have happened to anybody. And yet, due to the fact that such everyday events had been predicted about the Messiah **hundreds of years before the arrival of Jesus**, the fulfillment of the events becomes one of the most amazing miracles recorded in the Bible. It is no wonder that Jesus, the apostles, and the early church used fulfilled Messianic prophecy as one of its foundational pillars of proof and evangelistic tools.

APPEALING TO PROPHECY

Even a slight familiarity with the New Testament texts sufficiently demonstrates the idea that Jesus, the apostles, and the other New Testament writers used the Old Testament Messianic prophecies as one of their main apologetic tools to prove the deity and Messianic role of Jesus Christ.

The Writers of the Gospel Accounts Applied Messianic Prophecy to Jesus Christ

The gospel writers repeatedly peppered their narratives of the life and actions of Jesus Christ with allusions, quotes, and Messianic prophecies from the Old Testament, which they applied to Jesus. Matthew 1 includes the Messianic prophecy taken from Isaiah 7:14 in which a virgin was predicted to bear a son. Matthew applies this virgin-birth prophesy to the birth of Jesus Christ. In chapter 2, Matthew references Micah 5:2, in which the birth city of the Messiah was named, again applying the prophecy to Jesus. In Matthew 3, the Bible writer notes that John the Baptizer was the fulfillment of Isaiah's prophecy in 40:3, indicating that John was the forerunner of the Messiah which, again, is Jesus Christ. Matthew 4:15-16 references another Messianic prophecy that discusses the land of Zebulun and Naphtali, again applying the prophecy to Jesus Christ. Looking, then, at the first four chapters of the book of Matthew, one is forcefully struck with the fact that one of the Bible writer's primary apologetic tools used to confirm that Jesus was (and is) the Messiah was a fervent appeal to Messianic prophecy as fulfilled in the life and actions of Jesus. Furthermore, Matthew's pattern of applying Old Testament, Messianic prophecy to Jesus continues throughout the remainder of his account.

Mark's gospel account, although not as replete with such prophecies, nevertheless includes appeals to Messianic prophecy and applies those prophecies to Jesus. Mark chapter 1 begins with quotations from Malachi 3 and Isaiah 40 that predict the forerunner of the Messiah. Mark applied these passages to John the Baptizer as the forerunner of Jesus Christ. Furthermore, during the crucifixion account as recorded in Mark, the Bible writer noted that Jesus was crucified between two thieves, and then he commented, "So the Scripture was fulfilled which says, 'And He was numbered with the transgressors' " (15:28). In addition, Mark included instances in which Jesus applied Messianic prophecy to Himself.

As with Matthew and Mark, Luke and John also appealed to numerous Messianic prophecies as proof of the deity of Jesus Christ. Luke chapter three cites the prophecy from Isaiah 40 concerning the Messianic forerunner and applies it to John the Baptizer, the forerunner of Christ. John does the same in 1:23. During Jesus' triumphal entry into Jerusalem, John records that Jesus rode into the city sitting on a donkey. John then commented on the situation by saying: "as it is written: 'Fear not, daughter of Zion; behold, your King is coming, sitting on a donkey's colt' "

(12:14-15). His reference was a clear appeal to the Messianic nature of this prophecy found in Zechariah 9:9. Again, in John 12:37-38, the Bible writer refers to a Messianic prophecy in Isaiah 53:1, and applies its fulfillment to the ministry of Jesus. During the crucifixion of Christ, John records that the soldiers cast lots for Jesus' clothing. John then references Psalm 22:18 as a Messianic prophecy: "They divided My garments among them, and for my clothing they cast lots."

Only a few of the many Messianic prophetic references in the gospel accounts have been documented here. Yet, even with this small sampling, the reader is struck with the clear conclusion that the gospel writers appealed to Old Testament, Messianic prophecy as proof of the deity of Christ.

Jesus' Appeal to Prophecy as it Applied to Him

On multiple occasions, Jesus directed His listeners to certain Messianic Old Testament scriptures, and applied those scriptures to Himself. Luke records an incident in the life of Jesus in which He visited a synagogue on the Sabbath in His hometown of Nazareth. While in attendance there, Jesus read a passage from Isaiah 61:1-2, and commented to those in attendance that the particular Scripture He had just read was fulfilled in their hearing.

During His arrest in the Garden of Gethsemane, Jesus addressed those who had come to arrest Him, asking them why they did not apprehend Him while He was with them daily teaching in the temple. He then stated: "But the Scriptures must be fulfilled" (Mark 14:49). His statement implied that this deed they were doing was a fulfillment of Old Testament Scriptures as they related to His Messianic role.

Again, in Luke 24, the resurrected Jesus appeared to two of His disciples on the road to Emmaus. They treated Him as a stranger, because they did not recognize Him. Upon striking up a conversation with Jesus, they began to discuss the events of Christ's death and burial in Jerusalem only a few days earlier. After the disciples related the events of the women at the empty tomb, Jesus began to speak to them with these words: "O foolish ones, and slow of heart to believe in all that the prophets have spoken! Ought not the Christ to have suffered these things and to enter into His glory?" (Luke 24:25-26). The verse following Jesus' statement explains: "And beginning at Moses and all the Prophets, He expounded to them in all the Scriptures the things concerning Himself."

A few verses later, in the same chapter, Jesus appeared to several more of His disciples and applied the Old Testament prophecies to His activities again: "Then He said to them, 'These are the words which I spoke to you while I was still with you, that all the things must be fulfilled which were written in the Law of Moses and the Prophets and the Psalms concerning Me' " (Luke 24:44). Such statements made by Jesus show that one of the main lines of evidence that He used to establish His identity as the Messiah was the application of Old Testament Messianic prophecy to Himself.

Messianic Prophecy Applied to Jesus in the Book of Acts

The recorded writings and sermons of the apostles after the ascension of Jesus are replete with appeals to Messianic prophecy as proof of the Messianic identity of Jesus Christ. In the first recorded gospel sermon on the Day of Pentecost, Peter explained to those in Jerusalem that the resurrection of Christ was a fulfillment of the Messianic prophecy uttered by David in Psalm 16:8-11 (in which the Lord would not allow His Holy One to see corruption) and Psalm 110:1. In Acts 3, Peter addressed another multitude of those dwelling in Jerusalem. In his sermon, he stated: "But those things which God foretold by the mouth of all His prophets, that Christ would suffer, He has thus fulfilled" (vs. 18). In that same sermon, Peter referred his audience back to Deuteronomy 18, in which Moses had foretold the coming of a prophet like himself, which Peter applied to Jesus (as did Stephen in his sermon in Acts 7:37). In the next chapter, Peter is arrested and allowed to speak to the high priest and his family. In Peter's statements to these leaders, he again referred back to the Old Testament, quoted Psalm 118:22 about the stone that was rejected by the builders, and applied the prophecy to Jesus.

In one of the most memorable conversion accounts in Acts, Philip the evangelist was called to meet with an Ethiopian treasurer on the road to Gaza. As Philip approached, the Eunuch was reading a passage from Isaiah 53. Upon their meeting, the Eunuch asked Philip about the prophecy, wondering whether the prophet was speaking of himself or someone else. From that text, the Bible says that Philip preached Jesus to the Eunuch, applying the passage from Isaiah as a Messianic prophecy with its fulfillment in the person of Christ (Acts 8:26-40). In another memorable conversion account, Peter visited the house of Cornelius and preached the Gospel to him and all his household. Included in Peter's message was the following statement concerning Jesus: "To Him **all the prophets witness**, that through His name, whoever believes in Him will receive remission of sins" (Acts 10:43, emp. added).

As one continues through the book of Acts, it becomes evident that Paul often appealed to prophecy as evidence of Christ's deity. In Acts 13, while preaching to those in the synagogue in Antioch of Pisidia, he commented that those responsible for killing Jesus did so because they did not know "the voices of the Prophets which are read every Sabbath" (Acts 13:27). In the same verse he concluded that because of their ignorance of the prophetic message, the murderers of Christ actually fulfilled the prophecies concerning Jesus in their abuse of Him. Paul further quoted from Psalm 2:7, Isaiah 55:3, and Psalm 16:10, considering these Old Testament passages as Messianic prophecy and applying them to Jesus Christ. In a separate sermon, delivered much later, Paul stood before King Agrippa and told him that Jesus is the Christ. In his oratory to Agrippa, Paul acknowledged that the king was "expert in all customs and questions which have to do with the Jews" (Acts 26:3). Paul further noted that in his teachings concerning Jesus as the Messiah, he was saying to Agrippa "no other things than those which the prophets and Moses said would come" (26:22). In his concluding remarks, Paul said to the king, "King Agrippa, do you believe the prophets? I know that you do believe." Agrippa responded to Paul with these words: "You almost persuade me to become a Christian" (Acts 26:27-28).

Examples of Messianic prophecy applied to Jesus by the early propagators of Christianity as recorded in the book of Acts could easily be multiplied further. These few instances suffice to establish the fact that, throughout the book of Acts, predictive prophecy as it applied to Jesus as the Messiah stood as one of the foundational pillars upon which Christianity was based and spread.

Messianic Prophecy Applied to Jesus in the Epistles

Without providing an exhaustive study of every instance of Old Testament prophecy applied to Jesus in the epistles, this brief section will provide enough examples to establish the fact that the epistles, in similar fashion to the other books of the New Testament, rely heavily upon Messianic prophecy to establish the deity of Jesus Christ.

The book of Romans begins with a section discussing the Gospel of God, "which He promised before through His prophets in the Holy Scriptures, concerning His Son Jesus Christ our Lord, who was born of the seed of David according to the flesh..." (1:2-3). In the book of Galatians, Paul refers back to the promise made to Abraham, that through the seed of the patriarch all nations would be blessed. Paul then applies that promise to Jesus, stating that Jesus is the Seed of Abraham through whom the world would receive the blessing of Abraham (Galatians 3:15-18). The writer of the book of Hebrews opens his book discussing the merits of Christ, applying many Old Testament passages such as Psalm 2:7 and Psalm 110:1 to Jesus. In Hebrews 5, the writer argues the case that Jesus is a priest after the order of Melchizedek as prophesied in Psalm 110:4. He repeats these sentiments in 7:17 and 7:21.

The epistles of 1 and 2 Peter contain numerous examples of such prophetic application to Jesus. One of the most potent passages along these lines is found in 1 Peter 1:10-12:

> Of this salvation the prophets have inquired and searched carefully, who prophesied of the grace that would come to you, searching what, or what manner of time, the Spirit of Christ who was in them was indicating when He testified beforehand the sufferings of Christ and the glories that would follow. To them it was revealed that, not to themselves, but to us they were ministering the things which now have been reported to you through those who have preached the gospel to you by the Holy Spirit sent from heaven—things which angels desire to look into.

In 1 Peter 2:6, the apostle applies Isaiah 28:16 and Psalm 118:22 to Christ, describing Him as the chief cornerstone rejected by the builders. Again in 1 Peter 2:22, the apostle applies Isaiah 53:9 to Jesus, referring to the fact that the Messiah would be sinless as was Jesus.

It becomes readily obvious, then, that the New Testament writers and apostles frequently referred to Old Testament, Messianic prophecy and applied the fulfillment of such prophecies to the life, death, and resurrection of Christ. It is impossible to deny that one of the main lines of reasoning upon which the Christian faith was founded from its inception is the idea that Jesus Christ fulfilled the Old Testament prophecies that looked forward to a coming Messiah.

CONCLUSION

In the Old Testament, it is almost as if we have a satellite picture from space of the Messiah many thousands of miles away, yet with each new prophecy, the picture continues to move nearer, until at last we are able to view a complete close-up of the Messiah—Jesus Christ. As the distinguished Hebrew scholar Charles Briggs noted: "In Jesus of Nazareth the key of the Messianic prophecy of the Old Testament has been found. All its phases find their realization in His unique personality, in His unique work, and in His unique kingdom. The Messiah of prophecy appears in the Messiah of history" (1988, p. 498).

In Acts 8:26-40, Philip the evangelist approached the Ethiopian who was riding in a chariot reading the Old Testament Scriptures. As Philip approached, he heard the man reading a section from Isaiah 53 in which the sufferings of the Messiah are depicted. Upon entering into a conversation with Philip, the man asked Philip, "[O]f whom does the prophet say this, of himself or of some other man?" Immediately after this question, the Bible says that Philip "opened his mouth, and beginning at this Scripture, preached Jesus to him" (Acts 8:35). In truth, Jesus is the sum total of every Old Testament, Messianic prophecy ever uttered. From any single one of those ancient Scriptures, the honest, informed individual could open his or her mouth and preach Jesus, the Messiah.

CHAPTER 5

"THE VERY WORKS THAT I DO BEAR WITNESS OF ME"

The Bible begins with the miracle of Creation (Genesis 1:1), and ends with a reminder of the miraculous Second Coming of Christ (Revelation 22:20). Like polka dots on a Dalmatian, wondrous miracles wrought by God and His messengers spatter the biblical text. God created the Universe out of nothing (Genesis 1), and centuries later flooded the entire Earth with water (Genesis 7). He sent ten plagues upon the Egyptians (Exodus 7-12), parted the Red Sea (Exodus 14), and caused water to come from a rock twice during Israel's forty years of wandering in the wilderness (Exodus 17; Numbers 20). He healed a leper (2 Kings 5), raised many from the dead (1 Kings 17; Matthew 27:52-53), and on two different occasions translated men from Earth to heaven so that they never tasted death (Hebrews 11:5; 2 Kings 2:1-11). Even the Bible itself is the result of the miracle of God supernaturally guiding Bible writers in what they wrote. Rather than being the result of man's genius, the Bible claims to be "**God-breathed**" (2 Timothy 3:16, NIV). According to the apostle Peter, "[P]rophecy never had its origin in the will of man, but men spoke from God as they were **carried along by the Holy Spirit**" (2 Peter 1:21, NIV, emp. added). From revelation to inspiration, from God's Creation to Jesus' incarnation, miraculous (supernatural) explanations lay at the heart of numerous biblical (and historical) events.

Some people adamantly claim that any type of miracle is absolutely impossible. Why do they say "no" to miracles? There are many reasons, but perhaps most significant is that they do not believe that God exists (or that if He does, He does not intervene in the natural world). A person who believes that the Universe and its contents evolved through natural processes over billions of years cannot believe in miracles because he or she thinks that nothing exists outside of nature. As the late, eminent astronomer of Cornell University, Carl Sagan, put it: "The Cosmos is all that is or ever was or ever will be" (1980, p. 4). Since a miracle is an extraordinary event that demands a supernatural explanation, no such event ever could occur in a world where only natural forces operate. Once a person denies God and the miracle of Creation, then he or she is forced to deny that miracles of any kind can occur. Christians believe in miracles because they believe that God exists and that the Bible (which reports some of God's miracles) is His Word, whereas atheists reject miracles because they do not believe in a higher, supernatural Being.

Those who hold to an atheistic viewpoint are correct about one thing: If God does not exist (or as the deist believes, if He does exist, but is unwilling to intervene in His creation), then miracles cannot occur. On the other hand, if God does exist (and evidence indicates that He does—see Thompson, 2003), then miracles not only are possible, but also probable. It makes perfectly good sense to conclude that if God created the Universe, then on occasion He might intervene through supernatural acts (i.e., miracles) to accomplish His divine purposes.

MIRACULOUS CONFIRMATION

Since the world began, God has revealed messages to mankind "by the mouth of His holy prophets" (Luke 1:70; cf. Luke 11:49-51; Acts 3:21) and worked various miracles through them for the purpose of confirming His Divine will. God gave Moses the ability to turn a staff into a snake and water into blood in order that his hearers "may believe the message" that he spoke (Exodus 4:1-9). Fire from Heaven consumed an altar on Mount Carmel so that Israel might know the one true God and that His faithful prophet Elijah spoke on His behalf (1 Kings 18:36-39). Centuries later, as the apostles went about preaching the Gospel, Mark wrote that the Lord was "working with them and confirming the word through the accompanying signs" (16:20). According to the writer of Hebrews, the salvation "which at first began to be spoken by the Lord...was confirmed to us by those who heard Him" (2:3). God bore witness "with signs and wonders, with various miracles, and gifts of the Holy Spirit, according to His own will" (2:4). Indeed, throughout the Bible God's spokesmen worked miracles in order to validate their divine message.

In view of the fact that miracles have served as a confirmation of God's revelation since time began, it should be no surprise that "when the fullness of time had come" (Galatians 4:4), and the promised Messiah, the Son of God, came to Earth for the purpose of saving the world from sin (Luke 19:10; John 3:16), that He would confirm His identity and message by performing miracles. Centuries before the birth of Christ, the prophet Isaiah foretold of a time when "the eyes of the blind shall be opened, and the ears of the deaf shall be unstopped.... [T]he lame shall leap like a deer, and the tongue of the dumb sing" (35:5-6). Although this language has a figurative element to it, it literally is true of the coming of the Messiah. When John the Baptizer heard about the works of Christ, he sent two of his disciples to Jesus asking if He was "the Coming One" of Whom the prophets spoke. Jesus responded to John's disciples by pointing to the people whom He had miraculously healed (thus fulfilling Isaiah's Messianic prophecy), saying, "Go and tell John the things which you hear and see: the blind see and the lame walk; the lepers are cleansed and the deaf hear; the dead are raised up and the poor have the gospel preached to them" (Matthew 11:4-5; cf. Mark 7:37). Jesus wanted them to know that He was doing exactly what "the Coming One" was supposed to do (cf. Isaiah 53:4; Matthew 8:17), and what the Jews expected Him to do—perform miracles (John 7:31; cf. John 4:48; 1 Corinthians 1:22).

Jesus' miracles served a different purpose than those wrought by Moses, Elijah, or one of the New Testament apostles or prophets. Unlike all other miracle workers recorded in Scripture, Jesus actually claimed to be the prophesied Messiah, the Son of God, and His miracles were performed to prove both the truthfulness of His message **and** His divine nature. Whereas the apostles and prophets of the New Testament worked miracles to confirm their message that **Jesus** was the Son of God, Jesus performed miracles to bear witness that **He** was, in fact, the Son of God. In response to a group of Jews who inquired about whether or not He was the Christ, Jesus replied,

> I told you, and you do not believe. The works that I do in My Father's name, they bear witness of Me.... I and My Father are one.... If I do not do the works of My Father, do not believe Me; but if I do, though you do not believe Me, believe the works, that you may know and believe that the Father is in Me, and I in Him (John 10:25, 30,37-38).

Similarly, on another occasion Jesus defended His deity, saying, "[T]he works which the Father has given Me to finish—the very works that I do—bear witness of Me, that the Father has sent Me" (John 5:36). While on Earth, Jesus was "attested by God...with miracles and wonders and signs which God performed through Him" (Acts 2:22, NASB). And, according to the apostle John, "Jesus did many other signs in the presence of His disciples, which are not written in this book; but **these are written that you may believe that Jesus is the Christ, the Son of God,** and that believing you may have life in His name" (John 20:30-31, emp. added). As would be expected from the One Who claimed to be God incarnate (cf. John 1:1-3,14; 10:30), Scripture records that Jesus performed miracles throughout His ministry in an effort to provide sufficient proof of His divine message and nature.

REASONS TO BELIEVE IN THE MIRACLES OF JESUS

Regardless of how much credible evidence one is able to set forth in a discussion on the miracles of Christ, certain individuals will never be convinced that Jesus is the Son of God. The Bible makes clear that even a number of those in the first century who saw the miraculous works of Jesus firsthand were not persuaded that He was the promised Messiah (cf. Mark 6:6). Rather than fall at His feet and call him "Lord" (as did the blind man who was healed by Jesus—John 9:38), countless Jews refused to believe His claims of divinity. Instead, they attributed His works to Satan, and said things like, "He has Beelzebub," or "By the ruler of the demons He casts out demons" (Mark 3:22). In light of such reactions to Jesus' miracles by some of those who actually walked the Earth with Him 2,000 years ago, it should not be surprising that many alive today also reject Him as Lord and God. As previously stated, one of the main reasons for rejecting His deity and the miracles which the Bible claims that He worked is simply because many people deny God's existence (even in the face of the heavens declaring His handiwork—cf. Psalm 19:1) and the Bible's inspiration (which also has been demonstrated with an abundant amount of evidence—see Thompson, 2001). Obviously, if one refuses to accept these two foundational pillars of Christianity, he will never be convinced that Jesus worked miracles. Still, both theists and atheists should consider several of the following reasons as to why the miracles of Jesus are credible testimonies of His divine nature and teachings.

Countless Thousands Witnessed His Miracles

Aside from the fact that Jesus' miracles are recorded in the most historically documented ancient book in all of the world (see chapter two), which time and again has proven itself to be a reliable witness to history, it also is significant that Jesus' miracles were not done in some remote place on Earth with only a few witnesses. Instead, the miracles of Jesus were attested by **multitudes** of people all across Palestine throughout His ministry. Jesus began His miracles in Cana of Galilee by turning water into wine at a wedding feast in the presence of His disciples and other guests (John 2:1-11). [Considering how much wine was made after the hosts had already run out (approximately 120 gallons—2:6), it would appear there were many guests at the feast. Exactly how many witnessed the amazing feat, we are not told. But, the apostle John did record that "the servants who had drawn the water knew" of the miracle (2:9), as well as Jesus' disciples (2:11).] On more than one Sabbath day, Jesus performed miracles in Jewish synagogues where countless contemporaries gathered to study Scripture on their holy day (Mark 1:23-28; Mark 3:1-6). Jesus once healed a sick man at the Pool of Bethesda in Jerusalem where "**a great multitude**" of sick people had congregated (John 5:3), and He healed a paralytic in a Capernaum house **full** of "Pharisees and teachers of the law...who had come out of every town of Galilee, Judea, and Jerusalem" (Luke 5:17). The house was so crowded with people, in fact, that those who brought the paralytic could not even enter the house through the door. Instead, they uncovered part of the roof, and lowered him through the tiling. Matthew recorded how Jesus "saw a **great multitude**; and He was moved with compassion for them, and healed their sick" (14:14, emp. added). Then, later, He took five loaves of bread and two fish and miraculously fed **5,000 men, plus their women and children,** while afterwards taking up twelve baskets full of leftovers (Matthew 14:15-21; Mark 6:33:43; Luke 9:10-17; John 6:1-14). On another occasion, Jesus took "a few little fish...and seven loaves" of bread and fed **4,000 men, besides women and children** (Matthew 15:32-39).

Truly, countless thousands of Jesus' contemporaries witnessed His miracles on various occasions throughout His ministry. They were not hidden or performed in inaccessible locations incapable of being tested by potential followers. Rather, they were subjected to analysis by Jews and Gentiles, believers and unbelievers, friends and foes. They were evaluated in the physical realm by physical senses. When Peter preached to those who had put Jesus to death, he reminded them that Christ's identity had been proved "by miracles, wonders, and signs which God did through Him in your midst, **as you yourselves also know"** (Acts 2:22, emp. added). The Jews had witnessed Christ's miracles occurring among them while He was on the Earth. In the presence of many eyewitnesses, Jesus gave sight to the blind, healed lepers, fed thousands with a handful of food, and made the lame to walk.

The Enemies of Christ Attested to His Works

Interestingly, although many of Jesus' enemies who witnessed His miracles rejected Him as the Messiah and attempted to undermine His ministry, even they did not deny the miracles that He worked. After Jesus raised Lazarus from the dead in the presence of many Jews, "the chief priests and the Pharisees gathered a council and said, 'What shall we do? For **this Man works many signs**' " (John 11:47, emp. added). According to Luke, even King Herod had heard enough reports about Jesus to believe that He could perform "some miracle" in his presence (Luke 23:8). Once, after Jesus healed a blind, mute, demon-possessed man in the midst of multitudes of people, the Pharisees responded, saying, "This fellow does not cast out demons except by Beelzebub, the ruler of the demons" (Matthew 12:24). While many of Jesus' enemies did not confess belief in Him as being the heaven-sent, virgin-born, Son of God, but attributed His works as being from Satan, it is important to notice that they did not deny the supernatural wonders that He worked. In fact, they confessed that He worked a miracle by casting a demon from a man, while on another occasion they scolded him for healing on the Sabbath (cf. Luke 13:10-17).

Even when Jesus' enemies diligently investigated the miracles that He performed in hopes of discrediting Him, they still failed in their endeavors. The apostle John recorded an occasion when Jesus gave sight to a man born blind (John 9:7). After receiving his sight, neighbors and others examined him, inquiring how he was now able to see. Later he was brought to the Pharisees, and they scrutinized him. They questioned him about the One who caused him to see, and then argued among themselves about the character of Jesus. They called for the parents of the man who was blind, and questioned them about their son's blindness. Then they called upon the man born blind again, and a second time questioned him about how Jesus opened his eyes. Finally, when they realized the man would not cave in to their intimidating interrogation and say some negative thing about Jesus, "they cast him out" (9:34). They rejected him, and the One Who made him well. Yet, they were unable to deny the miracle that Jesus performed. It was known by countless witnesses that this man was born blind, but, after coming in contact with Jesus, his eyes were opened. The entire case was scrutinized thoroughly by Jesus' enemies, yet even they had to admit that Jesus caused the blind man to see (John 9:16-17,24,26). It was a fact, accepted, not by credulous youths, but by hardened, veteran enemies of Christ.

Furthermore, there were some of those among Jesus' strongest critics who eventually did come to believe, not simply in His miracles, but that the wonders He worked really were from Heaven. John hinted of this belief when he wrote about how there was a division among the Pharisees concerning whether Jesus was from God. One group asked, "How can a man who is a sinner (as some among the Pharisees alleged—KB/EL) do such signs?" (John 9:16). Nicodemus, who was a Pharisee and a ruler of the Jews, came to Jesus by night and confessed, saying, "Rabbi, we know that You are a teacher come from God; for no one can do these signs that You do unless God is with him" (John 3:2). Years later, after the establishment of the church, Luke recorded how "a great many of the priests were obedient to the faith" (Acts 6:7). Truly, even many of those who were numbered among Jesus' enemies at one time eventually confessed to His being the Son of God. Considering that positive testimony from hostile witnesses is the weightiest kind of testimony in a court of law, such reactions from Jesus' enemies are extremely noteworthy in a discussion on the miracles of Christ.

Multiple Attestation of Writers

The case built for the authenticity of Jesus' miracles is further strengthened by the fact that His supernatural works were recorded, not by one person, but by multiple independent writers. Even unbelievers admit that various miracles in Jesus' life (including His resurrection) were recorded by more than one writer (cf. Barker, 1992, p. 179; Clements, 1990, p. 193). If scholars of ancient history generally rendered facts "unimpeachable" when two or three sources are in agreement (see Maier, 1991, p. 197), then the multiple attestation of Jesus' miracles by Matthew, Mark, Luke, John, and Paul (cf. 1 Corinthians 15:1-8) is extremely impressive. Unlike Islam and Mormonism, each of which relies upon the accounts/writings of one alleged inspired man (Muhammad and Joseph Smith, respectively), Christianity rests upon the foundation of multiple writers. Consider also that certain miracles Jesus performed, specifically the feeding of the 5,000 and His resurrection, are recorded in all four gospel accounts. Furthermore, the writers' attestation of Jesus' life and miracles is similar enough so as not to be contradictory, but varied enough so that one cannot reasonably conclude that they participated in collusion in order to perpetrate a hoax. Truly, the fact that multiple writers attest to the factuality of Jesus' miracles should not be taken lightly and dismissed with a wave of the hand.

Interestingly, Bible writers were not alone in their attestation of the wonders that Jesus worked. The first-century Jewish historian, Josephus, mentioned Jesus as being One Who "was a doer of wonderful **works** (*paradoxa*)" and Who "drew over to him many of the

Jews, and many of the Gentiles" (18:3:3, emp. added). Josephus used this same Greek word (*paradoxa*) earlier when referring to Elijah and his "wonderful and surprising works by prophecy" (9:8:6). The only instance of this word in the New Testament is found in Luke's gospel account where those who had just witnessed Jesus heal a paralytic "were all seized with astonishment and began glorifying God; and they were filled with fear, saying, 'We have seen **remarkable things** (*paradoxa*) today' " (5:26, NASB, emp. added). A reference to Jesus' amazing works was also described in one section of the *Babylonian Talmud* (known as the *Sanhedrin Tractate*) where Jewish leaders wrote, "On the eve of the Passover Yeshu [Jesus—KB/EL] was hanged. For forty days before the execution took place, a herald went forth and cried, 'He is going forth to be stoned because **he has practiced sorcery** and enticed Israel to apostacy....' But since nothing was brought forward in his favour he was hanged on the eve of Passover" (Shachter, 1994, 43a). Even though the Talmud describes Jesus' amazing deeds as "sorcery," and although we may never know for certain whether Josephus truly believed Jesus could work legitimate miracles, both acknowledge that Jesus' life was characterized by remarkable wonders—testimony that would be expected from certain unbelievers who were attempting to explain away the supernatural acts of Christ.

Bible Writers Reported Facts—not Fairy Tales

It also is important to understand that the Bible writers insisted that their writings were not based on imaginary, nonverifiable people and events, but instead were grounded on solid historical facts (as has been confirmed time and again by the science of archaeology). The apostle Peter, in his second epistle to the Christians in the first century, wrote: "For we did not follow cunningly devised fables when we made known to you the power and coming of our Lord Jesus Christ, but were eyewitnesses of His majesty" (1:16). In a similar statement, the apostle John insisted: "That which was from the beginning, which we have heard, which we have seen with our eyes, which we have looked upon, and our hands have handled, concerning the Word of life...that which we have seen and heard we declare to you, that you also may have fellowship with us" (1 John 1:1,3). When Luke wrote his account of the Gospel of Christ, he specifically and intentionally crafted his introduction to ensure that his readers understood that his account was historical and factual:

> Inasmuch as many have taken in hand to set in order a narrative of those things which have been fulfilled among us, just as those who from the beginning were eyewitnesses and ministers of the word delivered them to us, it seemed good to me also, having had perfect understanding of all things from the very first, to write to you an orderly account, most excellent Theophilus, that you may know the certainty of those things in which you were instructed (Luke 1:1-4).

In a similar line of reasoning, Luke included in his introduction to the book of Acts the idea that Jesus, "presented Himself alive after His suffering by many infallible proofs, being seen by them during forty days and speaking of the things pertaining to the kingdom of God" (Acts 1:3). In addition, when the apostle Paul was arguing the case that Jesus Christ had truly been raised from the dead, he wrote that the resurrected Jesus

> was seen by Cephas, then by the twelve. After that He was seen by over five hundred brethren at once, of whom the greater part remain to the present, but some have fallen asleep. After that He was seen by James, then by all the apostles. Then last of all He was seen by me also, as by one born out of due time (1 Corinthians 15:5-8).

This handful of verses by Peter, Paul, John, and Luke, reveal that the Bible writers insisted with conviction that their writings were not mythical, but were based on factual events. Furthermore, they specifically documented many of the eye-witnesses who could testify to the accuracy of their statements. As Henry S. Curr remarked more than half a century ago,

> We are not asked to believe in myths and legends of the kind associated with paganism, classical and otherwise, nor in cunningly devised fables or old wives' tales. We are besought to accept sober stories of incidents which cannot be accounted for in any other way save that God was directly and intimately at work in the matter (1941, 98: 478).

The claim that the Bible is filled with miracle myths can be made, but it cannot be reasonably maintained. The evidence is overwhelming that the Bible writers understood and insisted that their information about Jesus and His miracles was accurate and factual, just as were all other details in their narratives and letters. Furthermore, their claim of factual accuracy has been verified time and again by the discipline of archaeology as well as by refutations of alleged discrepancies between the various writings and history.

Jesus' Signs were Many and Varied

Another characteristic of Jesus' miracles is that more than a few are recorded in Scripture. One is not asked to believe that Jesus is the Son of God because He performed one or two marvelous deeds during His lifetime. On the contrary, genuine "miracles cluster around the Lord Jesus Christ like steel shavings to a magnet" (Witmer, 1973, 130:132). The gospel accounts are saturated with a variety of miracles that Christ performed, not for wealth or political power, but that the world may be convinced that He was sent by the Father to bring salvation to mankind (cf. John 5:36; 10:37-38). As Isaiah prophesied, Jesus performed **miracles of healing** (Isaiah 53:4; Matthew 8:16-17). He cleansed a leper with the touch of His hand (Matthew 8:1-4), and healed all manner of sickness and disease with the word of His mouth (cf. John 4:46-54). One woman who had a hemorrhage for twelve years was healed immediately simply by touching the fringe of His garment (Luke 8:43-48). Similarly, on one occasion after Jesus came into the land of Gennesaret, **all** who were sick in **all** of the surrounding region came to Him, "and begged Him that they might only touch the hem of His garment. And as many as touched it were made perfectly well" (Matthew 14:34-36; Mark 3:10). Generally speaking, "**great multitudes** came to Him, having with them the lame, blind, mute, maimed, and many others; and they laid them down at Jesus' feet, and He healed them" (Matthew 15:30, emp. added). "He cured **many** of infirmities, afflictions...and to **many** blind He gave sight" (Luke 7:21, emp. added).

Even Jesus' enemies confessed to His **"many signs"** (John 11:48).

Jesus not only exhibited power over the sick and diseased, He also showed His **superiority over nature** more than once. Whereas God's prophet Moses turned water into blood by striking water with his rod (Exodus 7:20), Jesus simply willed water into wine at a wedding feast (John 2:1-11). He further exercised His power over the natural world by calming the Sea of Galilee during a turbulent storm (Matthew 8:23-27), by walking on water for a considerable distance to reach His disciples (Matthew 14:25-43), and by causing a fig tree to whither away at His command. In truth, Jesus' supernatural superiority over the physical world (which He created—Colossians 1:16) is exactly what we would expect from One Who claimed to be the Son of God.

Jesus' miracles were not limited to the natural world, however. As further proof of His deity, He also revealed His **power over the spiritual world** by casting out demons. "They brought to Him **many** who were demon-possessed. And He cast out the spirits with a word" (Matthew 8:16, emp. added). Luke also recorded that "He cured **many** of...evil spirits" (Luke 7:21, emp. added). Mark recorded where Jesus once exhibited power over a man overwhelmed with unclean spirits, which no one had been able to bind not even with chains and shackles; neither could anyone tame the demon-infested man (Mark 5:1-21). Jesus, however, cured him. Afterwards, witnesses saw the man with the unclean spirits "sitting at the feet of Jesus, clothed and in his right mind" (Luke 8:35-36). On several occasions, Jesus healed individuals who were tortured by evil spirits. And, "they were all amazed and spoke among themselves, saying, 'What a word this is! For with authority and power He commands the unclean spirits, and they come out'" (Luke 4:36).

Finally, Jesus even performed miracles that demonstrated His **power over death**. Recall that when John the Baptizer's disciples came to Jesus inquiring about His identity, Jesus instructed them to tell John that "the dead are raised" (Matthew 11:5). The widow of Nain's son had already been declared dead and placed in a casket when Jesus touched the open coffin and told him to "arise." Immediately, "he who was dead sat up and began to speak" (Luke 7:14-15). Lazarus had already been dead and buried for four days by the time Jesus raised him from the dead (John 11:1-44). Such a great demonstration of power over death caused "many of the Jews who had come to Mary, and had seen the things Jesus did" to believe in Him (John 11:45). What's more, Jesus' own resurrection from the dead was the climax of all of His miracles, and serves as perhaps the most convincing miracle of all (see chapter six).

In all, the Gospel records contain some thirty-seven specific supernatural acts that Jesus performed. If that number were to include such miracles as His virgin birth and transfiguration, and the multiple times He exemplified the ability to "read minds" and to know the past or future without having to learn of them through ordinary means (cf. John 4:15-19; 13:21-30; 2:25), etc., the number would reach upwards to fifty. Indeed, the miracles of Christ were varied and numerous. He healed the blind, lame, sick, and leprous, as well as demonstrated power over nature, demons, and death. The apostle John, who recorded the miracles of Christ "that you may believe that Jesus is the Christ, the Son of God, and that believing you may have life in His name" (John 20:31), also commented on how "Jesus did **many other** signs in the presence of His disciples, which are not written in this book" (20:30, emp. added). In fact, Jesus worked so many miracles throughout His ministry on Earth that, "if they were written one by one, I suppose that even the world itself could not contain the books that would be written" (John 21:25).

Power over Affliction	Cited In
Royal official's son	John 4:46-54
Peter's mother-in-law	Matthew 8:14-18; Mark 1:29-34; Luke 4:38-41
Leper	Matthew 8:1-4; Mark 1:40-45; Luke 5:12-14
Paralytic	Matthew 9:1-8; Mark 2:3-12; Luke 5: 18-26
Lame man at the Pool of Bethesda	John 5:1-16
Man with withered hand	Matthew 12:9-14; Mark 3:1-6; Luke 6: 6-11
Paralyzed centurion's servant	Matthew 8:5-13; Luke 7:1-10
Hemorrhaging woman	Matthew 9:20-22; Mark 5:25-34; Luke 8:43-48
Two blind men	Matthew 9:27-31
Deaf and mute man	Matthew 15:29-31; Mark 7:31-37
Blind man outside of Bethesda	Mark 8:22-26
Ten lepers	Luke 17:11-19
Man born blind	John 9
Crippled woman	Luke 13:10-17
Man with dropsy	Luke 14:1-6
Two blind men near Jericho	Matthew 20:29-34; Mark 10:46-52
Malchus' ear	Luke 22:50-51

"The Very Works that I Do Bear Witness of Me"

Power over Nature	Cited In
Water changed into wine	John 2:1-11
First catch of fish	Luke 5:1-7
Calming a turbulent storm	Matthew 8:23-27; Mark 4:36-41; Luke 8:22-25
Feeding 5,000	Matthew 14:15-21; Mark 6:30-34; Luke 9:10-17; John 6:1-14
Walking on water	Matthew 14:22-32; Mark 6:45-46; John 6:15-21
Feeding 4,000	Matthew 15:32-39; Mark 8:1-9
Money in the fish's mouth	Matthew 17:24-27
Fig tree withers	Matthew 21:18-22; Mark 11:12-14, 20-24
Second catch of fish	John 21:1-11

Power over Demons	Cited In
Man in synagogue at Capernaum	Mark 1:23-28; Luke 4:33-37
Mute, demon-possessed man	Matthew 9:32-34
Mary Magdalene	Luke 8:2
Two men at Gadara	Matthew 8:28-34; Mark 5:1-21; Luke 8:26-40
Blind, mute, demon-possessed man	Matthew 12:22-30; Mark 3:22-30; Luke 11:14-23
Syro-Phoenician's daughter	Matthew 15:21-28; Mark 7:24-30
Epileptic, demon-possessed child	Matthew 17:14-21; Mark 9:14-29; Luke 9:37-43

Power over Death	Cited In
Widow of Nain's son	Luke 7:11-18
Jairus' daughter	Matthew 9:18-19,23-26; Mark 5:21-24,35-43; Luke 8:40-42,49-56
Lazarus	John 11
Jesus' own resurrection	Matthew 28; Mark 16; Luke 24; John 20

The Miracles of Jesus were neither Silly nor Overboard

Admittedly, for some, a number of the miracles that Jesus performed are more easily accepted than others. The fact that a group of fishermen let their nets down into the sea and caught so many fish that the netting began to break (Luke 5:1-11) is not difficult for critics to accept (although not as a miracle). The idea of Jesus raising Lazarus from the dead after already being in the tomb for four days, however, is much harder for skeptics to believe. But, neither this miracle nor any other that Jesus worked is unworthy of our consideration because it is silly or overboard. People may reject the miracles of Christ because of their disbelief in the supernatural altogether, or because of their inability to attach naturalistic explanations to various miracles. However, they cannot be denied on the grounds that they are characterized by the absurd or ridiculous—that they are not. As Furman Kearley once stated, "The gospel records are marked by restraint and sublimity in the description of miracles" (1976, 93[27]:4).

The miracles of Christ certainly were **extra**ordinary (otherwise they would not be miracles), yet they were performed (and recorded) with all sanity and sobriety—exactly what one would expect if they really were signs from God. After all, He

> is the author and finisher of that unspeakable machine which we call the universe, ever working in accordance with its constitution on the strictest principles of law and order, and thus proclaiming that its Architect is no capricious being but one whose mental attributes are as mar-

> velous as His moral and spiritual qualities. In these circumstances, it would be very strange if the Biblical miracles represented the contradiction of orderly things (Curr, 1941, 98:471).

Since the omnipotent God has chosen to **control** His infinite power, and to use it in **orderly** and **rational** ways, one would expect that when God put on flesh (John 1:1-3,14) and exerted His supernatural power on Earth, it likewise would be characterized as power under control—miracles performed with infinite sobriety and rationality.

Unlike the stories of many alleged miracle workers from the past (or present), Jesus' miracles are characterized by restraint and dignity. Consider the miracle that Jesus performed on Malchus, a man who was about to arrest Jesus. Instead of doing something like commanding the left ear of Malchus to whither or fall off (after Peter severed his right one with a sword), Jesus simply touched the detached ear "and healed him" (Luke 22:51). A man who was about to turn Jesus over to His enemies has his ear cut off with a sword, and Jesus simply (yet miraculously) puts his ear back in place. What's more, that is all any Bible writer wrote about the matter. An amazing miracle was worked the night before Jesus' death, and the only thing revealed is that Jesus "touched his ear and healed him." As with all of Jesus' miracles,

> [t]here is no attempt to magnify the supernatural features of the incident. The happening is left to speak for itself. If truth be best unadorned, then there are no more effective illustrations of that doctrine than the Biblical records of signs and wonders. The writers do not dwell upon them. They rather take the marvels in their stride. They

> tell the story as succinctly as they can, and then pass on to deal with something else. That is exemplified very clearly in the Synoptic Gospels. We are told of the moral and physical miracle wrought in a house at Capernaum when four men bore a sick friend to the feet of Jesus, having removed part of the roof and lowered the pallet through the aperture. The man's sins were forgiven. This was a sign from heaven if there ever was one. His infirmity was also removed and that was another demonstration of our Lord's claims to be God manifest in the flesh. Matthew then proceeds to recount his call to discipleship and what followed. Procedure like that is repeated again and again. The writers do not linger over the supernatural as a modern novelist might do. The miracle is mentioned at greater or less length, and then the narrative goes on its way. It is true that reference is often made to the amazement created in the crowds which witnessed these mighty works of God; but even that is not emphasized inordinately (Curr, 1941, 98:473).

Furthermore, unlike those in other writings, Jesus' miracles were not characterized by the sorcerer's hocus pocus. In fact, there are few parallels to Jesus and the magicians of the ancient world. Even Rudolf Bultmann, the twentieth-century German writer who sought to explain away the miracles of Jesus, admitted that "the New Testament miracle stories are extremely reserved in this respect, since they hesitate to attribute to the person of Jesus the magical traits which were often characteristic of the Hellenistic miracle worker" (as quoted in Habermas, 2001, p. 113). Jesus could have performed any miracle that He wanted. He could have pulled rabbits from hats for the sole purpose of amusing people. He could have turned His Jewish enemies into stones, or given a person three eyes. He could have turned boys into men. He could have lit the robes of the Pharisees on fire and told them that hell would be ten times as hot. He could have formed a dozen sparrows out of clay as a child, and then, in the midst of a group of boys, turned the clay birds into live ones at the clap of His hands, as is alleged in the non-inspired apocryphal book, the *Gospel of Thomas* (1:4-9; *The Lost Books...*, 1979, p. 60). Certainly, Jesus **could** have done any number of silly, outlandish miracles. But, He didn't. In contrast to the miracles recorded in any number of non-inspired sources, Jesus' miracles were not characterized by

> endless tales of wonders with which literature and folklore of the world abounds. There is no suggestion of magic or legerdemain about the mighty works of God described in the Bible. On the contrary, they are invariably characterized by a sanity and sobriety and reasonableness.... There is nothing extravagant or bizarre about them.... When the miracles of our Lord which are described in the four Gospels are compared with those derived from other sources, the difference is like that of chalk and cheese" (Curr, 98:471-472).

Jesus Worked Wonders that are not Being Duplicated Today

Finally, neither the modern alleged "faith healer" nor the twenty-first-century scientist is duplicating the miracles that Jesus worked while on Earth 2,000 years ago. Pseudo-wonder workers today stage seemingly endless events where willing participants with supposed sicknesses appear and act as if they are being healed of their diseases by the laying on of hands. Nebulous aches and pains and dubious illnesses that defy medical substantiation are supposedly cured by prominent "faith healers" who simultaneously are building financial empires with the funds they receive from gullible followers. Frauds like Oral Roberts, Benny Hinn, and a host of others have made many millions of dollars off of viewers who naively send them money without stopping to consider the real differences between the miracles that Jesus worked and what they observe these men do today.

Jesus went about "healing **every** sickness and **every** disease" (Matthew 9:35, emp. added). His miraculous wonders knew no limitations. He could cure anything. Luke, the learned physician (Colossians 4:14), recorded how He could restore a shriveled hand in the midst of His enemies (Luke 6:6-10), and heal a severed ear with the touch of His hand (Luke 22:51). He healed "many" of their blindness (Luke 7:21), including one man who had been **born** blind (John 9:1-7)! What's more, He even raised the dead simply by calling out to them (John 11:43). What modern-day "spiritualist," magician, or scientist has come close to doing these sorts of things that defy natural explanations? Who is going into schools for the blind and giving children their sight? Who is going to funerals or graveyards to raise the dead? These are the kinds of miracles that Jesus worked—supernatural feats that testify to His identity as the heaven-sent Savior of the world.

CONCLUSION

As should be expected from the One Who claimed to be God incarnate (cf. John 1:1-3,14; 10:30), Scripture records that Jesus performed miracles throughout His ministry in order to provide sufficient proof of His divine message and nature. Countless thousands witnessed His miracles. He performed them throughout His ministry—miracles that in a host of ways are unlike the alleged wonders worked by sorcerers, scientists, or "spiritualists" of the past or present. Even Jesus' enemies attested to the wonders that He worked, which later were recorded, not by one person, but by multiple independent writers who were dedicated to reporting facts rather than fairy tales.

Jesus worked miracles, not for the sake of entertaining individuals or in order to make a profit off of His audiences, but that the world may know that Jesus and God are one (John 10:30,38), and that the Father sent Him to Earth to save mankind from sin (John 5:36). He "did many other signs in the presence of His disciples, which are not written in this book; but **these are written that you may believe that Jesus is the Christ, the Son of God,** and that believing you may have life in His name" (John 20:30-31, emp. added). Certainly, among the greatest proofs for the deity of Christ are the miracles that He worked.

CHAPTER 6

JESUS CHRIST—DEAD OR ALIVE?

In all likelihood, some people who read this book will already have made up their minds about the resurrection of Jesus Christ. And, many probably acknowledge that Jesus Christ lived on this Earth for approximately 33 years, died at the hand of the Roman procurator, Pontius Pilate, was buried in a new tomb owned by Joseph of Arimathea, and miraculously defeated death by His resurrection three days later.

But there may be some who have lingering doubts about the truthfulness of the resurrection of Christ. In fact, many people have much more than lingering doubts; they already have made up their minds that the story of the resurrection happened too long ago, was witnessed by too few people, has not been proven scientifically, and thus should be discarded as an unreliable legend.

Regardless of which position best describes your personal view of Christ's resurrection, what we all must do is check our prejudice at the door, and be willing openly and honestly to examine the historical facts attending the resurrection.

FACT: JESUS CHRIST LIVED AND DIED

Determining whether Jesus Christ actually lived is something that needs to be established before one can begin to discuss His resurrection. Obviously, if it cannot be proved beyond reasonable doubt that He did walk this Earth, then any discussion about whether or not He rose from the dead digresses quickly into an exercise in myth making based on little more than guesswork and human imagination. Fortunately, the fact that Jesus lived is almost universally accepted since, as we documented in chapter one, a host of hostile witnesses testified of His life, and the New Testament documents in intricate detail His existence. [Even if one does not accept the New Testament as inspired of God, he or she cannot deny that its books contain historical information regarding a person by the name of Jesus Christ Who really did live in the first century A.D.] The honest historian is forced to admit that documentation for the existence and life of Jesus runs deep and wide. Thus, knowing that Jesus Christ existed allows us to move farther into the subject of His resurrection.

For most people, coming to the conclusion that Jesus died is not difficult, due to either of two reasons. First, the Bible believer accepts the fact that Jesus died because several different biblical writers confirm it. Second, the unbeliever accepts the idea, based not upon biblical evidence, but rather on the idea that the natural order of things that he has experienced in this life is for a person to live and eventually die. Once evidence sufficient to prove Christ's existence in history has been established, the naturalist/empiricist has no trouble accepting His death. However, in order to provide such people with a few more inches of common ground on this matter, it would be good to note that several secular writers substantiated the fact that Jesus Christ did die. Tacitus, the ancient Roman historian writing in approximately A.D. 115, documented Christ's physical demise when he wrote concerning the Christians that "their originator, Christ, had been executed in Tiberius' reign by the governor of Judea, Pontius Pilatus" (1952, 15.44).

In addition to Roman sources, early Jewish rabbis whose opinions are recorded in the Talmud acknowledged the death of Jesus. According to the earlier rabbis,

> Jesus of Nazareth was a transgressor in Israel who practised magic, scorned the words of the wise, led the people astray, and said that he had not come to destroy the law but to add to it. He was hanged on Passover Eve for heresy and misleading the people (Bruce, 1953, p. 102, emp. added).

Likewise, Jewish historian Josephus wrote:

> [T]here arose about this time Jesus, a wise man.... And when Pilate had condemned him to the cross on his impeachment by the chief men among us, those who had loved him at first did not cease (*Antiquities of the Jews*, 18.3.3).

The fact that Pilate condemned Christ to the cross is an undisputed historical fact. As archaeologist Edwin Yamauchi stated:

> Even if we did not have the New Testament or Christian writings, we would be able to conclude from such non-Christian writings such as Josephus, the Talmud, Tacitus, and Pliny the Younger that ...he root Pilate in the reign of Tiberius (1995, p. 222).

There are still those who, in an attempt to deny the bodily resurrection of Christ, have suggested that **Christ did not die at the time of the crucifixion**. Rather, it is alleged, the Lord merely "swooned" upon the cross. Some claim that He later recovered from His ordeal and announced His resurrection! This concept appears to have been advanced first in 1768 by Peter Annet, an English deist. In 1977, Andreas Faber-Kaiser, a philosopher and journalist, advanced the notion that Jesus survived the ordeal of Calvary. The most prominent defender of this concept within recent years has been Hugh Schonfield. His book, *The Passover Plot*, has been on the market for forty years (having gone through twenty printings in its first decade alone!). Schonfield theorized that Jesus, believing Himself to be the Messiah, plotted to feign His own "death," intending, after the dramatic event, to sweep triumphantly into power. Note his assertion: "He [Christ] plotted and schemed with the utmost skill and resourcefulness, sometimes making secret arrangements, taking advantage of every circumstance conducive to the attainment of His objectives" (1965, p. 155). Schonfield alleged that the sponge offered to Jesus while on the cross (John 19:29-30) was soaked with a powerful narcotic, the purpose of which was to induce the appearance of death. The plan was that friends would remove His body and hide Him until He could regain His strength. According to Schonfield, however, the plot was foiled when the Roman soldier unexpectedly thrust a spear into Jesus' side. The Lord supposedly was removed from the cross unconscious, and was taken to a secret place where He subsequently expired and was quietly buried.

As often is so typical of such "scholars," Schonfield plays havoc with the New Testament records that deal with the post-resurrection appearances of Christ. For example, he argues that the man who appeared to Mary Magdalene in the garden (John 20:11ff.) was not Jesus Himself, as the apostle records, but probably one of Christ's co-conspirators—perhaps the man who gave the Lord the drug at the cross (pp. 168-169). The manner in which infidels deal with the biblical text is fascinating. Schonfield would not even know of that garden interview but for John's account; he thus accepts that as historical. At the same time he presumes to inform us—nineteen centuries this side of the event, mind you—that John's identification of the man as Jesus is not reliable! In view of such manipulations, it is not surprising that even a modernistic writer would admit: "The swoon theory is very ingenious, but it rides roughshod over all evidence from the Christian sources so much so that there was no hint of this theory by any of the early opponents of Christianity" (Cornfield, 1982, p. 182).

One of the main tenets of the Gospel is this: "Christ **died** for our sins according to the scriptures" (1 Corinthians 15:3). Honest men and women, exposed to the evidence, must admit the validity of this fact.

FACT: THE TOMB OF CHRIST WAS EMPTY

Around the year A.D. 165, Justin Martyr penned his *Dialogue with Trypho.* At the beginning of chapter 108 of this work, he recorded a letter that the Jewish community had been circulating concerning the empty tomb of Christ:

> A godless and lawless heresy had sprung from one Jesus, a Galilaean deceiver, whom we crucified, but his disciples stole him by night from the tomb where he was laid when unfastened

> from the cross, and now deceive men by asserting that he has risen from the dead and ascended to heaven.

Somewhere around the sixth century, another caustic treatise written to defame Christ circulated among the Jewish community. In this narrative, known as *Toledoth Yeshu*, Jesus was described as the illegitimate son of a soldier named Joseph Pandera. He also was labeled as a disrespectful deceiver who led many away from the truth. Near the end of the treatise, under a discussion of His death, the following paragraph can be found:

> A diligent search was made and he [Jesus—KB/EL] was not found in the grave where he had been buried. A gardener had taken him from the grave and had brought him into his garden and buried him in the sand over which the waters flowed into the garden (*Toledoth Yeshu*).

Upon reading Justin Martyr's description of one Jewish theory regarding the tomb of Christ, and another premise from *Toledoth Yeshu*, it becomes clear that a single common thread unites them both—the tomb of Christ had no body in it!

All parties involved recognized the fact that Christ's tomb laid empty on the third day. Feeling compelled to give reasons for this unexpected vacancy, Jewish authorities apparently concocted several different theories to explain the body's disappearance. The most commonly accepted one seems to be that the disciples of Jesus stole His body away by night while the guards slept (Matthew 28:13). Yet, how could the soldiers identify the thieves if they had been asleep? And why were the sentinels not punished by death for sleeping on the job and thereby losing their charge (cf. Acts 12:6-19)? And an even more pressing question comes to mind—why did the soldiers need to explain anything if a body was still in the tomb?

When Peter stood up on the Day of Pentecost after the resurrection of Christ, the crux of his sermon rested on the facts that Jesus died, was buried, and rose again on the third day. In order to silence Peter, and stop a mass conversion, the Jewish leaders needed simply to produce the body of Christ. Why did the Jewish leaders not take the short walk to the garden and produce the body? Simply because they could not; the tomb was empty—a fact the Jews recognized and tried to explain away. The apostles knew it, and preached it boldly in the city of Jerusalem. And thousands of inhabitants of Jerusalem knew it and converted to Christianity. John Warwick Montgomery accurately assessed the matter when he wrote: "It passes the bounds of credibility that the early Christians could have manufactured such a tale and then preached it among those who might easily have refuted it simply by producing the body of Jesus" (1964, p. 78).

The tomb of Jesus was empty, and that is a fact.

FACT: THE APOSTLES PREACHED THAT JESUS PHYSICALLY ROSE FROM THE DEAD

Regardless of whether or not one believes that Christ rose from the dead, one thing that cannot be denied is the fact His apostles preached that they saw Jesus after He physically rose from the dead. The New Testament book of Acts stresses this issue almost to the point of redundancy. Acts 1:22, as one example, finds

Peter and the other apostles choosing an apostle who was to "become a witness" of the resurrection of Christ. Then, on the Day of Pentecost, Peter insisted in his sermon to the multitude that had assembled to hear him that "God raised up" Jesus and thus loosed Him from the pangs of death (Acts 2:24). And to make sure that his audience understood that it was a physical resurrection, Peter stated specifically that Jesus' "flesh did not see corruption" (Acts 2: 31). His point was clear: Jesus had been physically raised from the dead and the apostles had witnessed the resurrected Christ. [Other passages which document that the central theme of the apostles' preaching was the bodily resurrection of Christ include Acts 3:15, 3:26, 4:2,10,33, and 5:30.] Furthermore, the entire chapter of 1 Corinthians 15 (especially verse 14) verifies that the preaching of the apostle Paul centered on the resurrection.

Even Joseph McCabe, one of the early twentieth century's most outspoken infidels, remarked: "Paul was absolutely convinced of the resurrection; and this proves that it was widely believed not many years after the death of Jesus" (1926, p. 24). The skeptical modernist Shirley Jackson Case of the University of Chicago was forced to concede: "The testimony of Paul alone is sufficient to convince us, beyond any reasonable doubt, that this was the commonly accepted opinion in his day—an opinion at that time supported by the highest authority imaginable, the eye-witnesses themselves" (1909, pp. 171-172). C.S. Lewis correctly stated: "In the earliest days of Christianity an 'apostle' was first and foremost a man who claimed to be an eyewitness of the Resurrection" (1975, p. 188).

It has been suggested by some critics that the apostles and other witnesses did not actually see Christ, but merely hallucinated. However, Gary Habermas had this to say about such a fanciful idea:

> [H]allucinations are comparably rare. They're usually caused by drugs or bodily deprivation. Chances are, you don't know anybody who's ever had a hallucination not caused by one of those two things. Yet we're supposed to believe that over a course of many weeks, people from all sorts of backgrounds, all kinds of temperaments, in various places, all experienced hallucinations? That strains the hypothesis quite a bit, doesn't it? (as quoted in Strobel, 1998, p. 239).

Indeed, the hallucination theory is a feeble attempt to undermine the fact that the apostles (and other first-century eyewitnesses of a risen Christ) preached the message that they really had seen a resurrected Jesus.

The apostles preached that Christ physically rose, and those who heard the apostles verified that they preached the resurrection. Apart from what a person believes about the resurrection of Christ, he or she cannot deny (legitimately) the fact that the apostles traveled far and wide to preach one central message—the death, burial, and resurrection of Jesus Christ.

FACT: THE APOSTLES SUFFERED AND DIED BECAUSE OF THEIR TEACHINGS ABOUT THE RESURRECTION

As the list of facts continues, one that must be enumerated is the verified historical fact that the majority of the apostles suffered cruel, tortuous deaths because they preached that Christ rose from the dead. Documenting these persecutions is no difficult task. *Fox's Book of Martyrs* relates that Paul was beheaded, Peter was crucified (probably upside down), Thomas was thrust through with a spear, Matthew was slain with a halberd, Matthias was stoned and beheaded, Andrew was crucified, and the list proceeds to describe the martyr's death of every one of the Lord's faithful apostles except John the brother of James (Forbush, 1954, pp. 2-5).

Additional testimony comes from the early church fathers. Eusebius, who was born about A.D. 260 and died about 340, wrote that Paul was beheaded in Rome and that Peter was crucified there (*Ecclesiastical History*, 2.25). [Exactly how and where Peter was martyred is unclear from history; the fact that he was martyred is not.] Clement of Rome (who died about A.D. 100), in chapter five of his *First Epistle to the Corinthians*, also mentioned the martyrs' deaths of Peter and Paul. Luke, the writer of the book of Acts, documented the death of James when he stated: "Now about that time Herod the king stretched out his hand to harass some from the church. Then he killed James the brother of John with the sword" (Acts 12:1-2). The apostle Paul perhaps summed it up best when he said:

> For I think that God has displayed us, the apostles, last, as men condemned to death; for we have been made a spectacle to the world, both to angels and to men. We are fools for Christ's sake, but you are wise in Christ! We are weak, but you are strong! You are distinguished, but we are dishonored! To the present hour we both hunger and thirst, and we are poorly clothed, and beaten, and homeless. And we labor, working with our

> own hands. Being reviled, we bless; being persecuted, we endure; being defamed, we entreat. We have been made as the filth of the world, the offscouring of all things until now (1 Corinthians 4:9-13).

Wayne Jackson correctly noted that "while men may die out of religious deception, they do not willingly go to their deaths knowing they are perpetrating a hoax" (1982, 1:34).

Some ill-advised attempts have been made to deny that Christ's apostles actually died because of their belief in, and preaching of, the resurrection. For example, it has been proposed that the apostles died because they were political instigators or rabble-rousers. However, combining the high moral quality of their teachings with the testimony of the early church fathers, and acknowledging the fact that their primary task was to be witnesses of the resurrection, it is historically inaccurate to imply that the apostles suffered for any reason other than their confession of the resurrection. The fact of the matter is, the apostles died because they refused to stop preaching that they had seen the Lord alive after His death.

FACT: THE BIBLE IS THE MOST HISTORICALLY ACCURATE BOOK OF ANTIQUITY

Sir William Ramsay was a one-time unbeliever and world-class archaeologist. His extensive education had ingrained within him the keenest sense of scholarship. But along with that scholarship came a built-in prejudice about the supposed inaccuracy of the Bible (specifically the book of Acts). As Ramsay himself remarked:

> [A]bout 1880 to 1890, the book of the Acts was regarded as the weakest part of the New Testament. No one that had any regard for his reputation as a scholar cared to say a word in its defence. The most conservative of theological scholars, as a rule, thought the wisest plan of defence for the New Testament as a whole was to say as little as possible about the Acts (1915, p. 38).

As could be expected of someone who had been trained by such "scholars," Ramsay held the same view. He eventually abandoned it, however, because he was willing to do what few people of his time dared to do—explore the Bible lands themselves with an archaeologist's pick in one hand and an open Bible in the other. His self-stated intention was to prove the inaccuracy of Luke's history as recorded in the book of Acts. But, much to his surprise, the book of Acts passed every test that any historical narrative could be asked to pass. In fact, after years of literally digging through the evidence in Asia Minor, Ramsay concluded that Luke was an exemplary historian. Lee S. Wheeler, in his classic work, *Famous Infidels Who Found Christ*, recounted Ramsay's life story in great detail (1931, pp. 102-106), and then quoted the famed archaeologist, who ultimately admitted:

> The more I have studied the narrative of the Acts, and the more I have learned year after year about Graeco-Roman society and thoughts and fashions, and organization in those provinces, the more I admire and the better I understand. I set out to look for truth on the borderland where Greece and Asia meet, and found it here [in the

> book of Acts—KB/EL]. You may press the words of Luke in a degree beyond any other historian's, and they stand the keenest scrutiny and the hardest treatment, provided always that the critic knows the subject and does not go beyond the limits of science and of justice (Ramsay, 1915, p. 89).

In his book, *The Bearing of Recent Discovery on the Trustworthiness of the New Testament*, Ramsay was constrained to admit: "Luke is a historian of the first rank; not merely are his statements of fact trustworthy, he is possessed of the true historic sense.... In short, this author should be placed along with the very greatest historians" (1915, p. 222; cf. also Ramsay's 1908 work, *Luke the Physician*). (NOTE: For more extensive information on the reliability of the New Testament records, refer back to chapter 2).

Please note, however, that this argument is not being introduced here to claim that the New Testament is inspired (although certain writers have used it in this way quite effectively). Rather, it is inserted at this point in the discussion to illustrate that the books which talk the most about the resurrection have proven to be accurate when confronted with any verifiable fact. Travel to the Bible Lands and see for yourself if you doubt biblical accuracy. Carry with you an honest, open mind and an open Bible, and you will be forced to respect the New Testament writers as accurate historians.

ON SUPPOSED CONTRADICTIONS WITHIN THE GOSPELS

Maybe the New Testament documents are accurate when they discuss historical and geographical information. But what about all the alleged "contradictions" among the gospel accounts of the resurrection? Charles Templeton, who worked for many years with the Billy Graham Crusade but eventually abandoned his faith, used several pages of his book, *Farewell to God*, to compare and contrast the statements within the four gospels, and then concluded: "The entire resurrection story is not credible" (1996, p. 122). Another well-known preacher-turned-skeptic, Dan Barker, has drawn personal delight in attempting to locate contradictions within the four accounts of the resurrection. In his book, *Losing Faith in Faith*, he filled seven pages with a list of the "contradictions" he believes he has uncovered. Eventually he stated: "Christians, either tell me exactly what happened on Easter Sunday, or let's leave the Jesus myth buried" (1992, p. 181).

It is interesting, is it not, that Barker demands to know "exactly what happened" on a day in ancient history that occurred almost 2,000 years ago? Such a request speaks loudly of the historical legitimacy of the resurrection story, since no other day in ancient history ever has been examined with such scrutiny. Historians today cannot tell "exactly what happened" on July 4, 1776 or April 12, 1861, yet Christians are expected to provide the "exact" details of Christ's resurrection? Fortunately, the gospel writers described "exactly what happened"—without contradiction. Examine the following evidence.

HEAD-ON COLLUSION

"Collusion: A secret agreement between two or more parties for a fraudulent, illegal, or deceitful purpose" (*The American Heritage*..., 2000, p. 363). Even if we never had heard the word collusion before, most of us still would understand the situation it describes. Suppose, for example, that five bank robbers don their nylon-hose masks, rob the city bank, and stash the cash in a nearby cave. Each robber then goes back to his respective house until the police search is concluded. The first robber hears a knock at his door and, upon opening it, finds a policeman who "just wants to ask him a few questions." The officer then inquires, "Where were you, and what were you doing, on the night of February 1, 2002?" The thief promptly responds, "I was at Joe Smith's house watching television with four other friends." The policeman obtains the four friends' names and addresses and visits each one of their homes. Every single robber, in turn, tells exactly the same story. Was it true? Absolutely not! But did the stories all sound exactly the same, with seemingly no contradictions? Yes.

Now, let's examine this principle in light of our discussion of the resurrection. If every single narrative describing the resurrection sounded exactly the same, what do you think would be said about those narratives? "They must have copied each other!" In fact, in other areas of Christ's life besides the resurrection, when the books of Matthew and Luke give the same information as the book of Mark, critics today claim that Matthew and Luke must have copied Mark because it is thought to be the earliest of the three books. Another raging question in today's upper echelons of biblical "scholarship" is whether Peter copied Jude in 2 Peter 2:4-17 (or whether Jude copied Peter), because the two segments of scripture sound so similar.

Amazingly, however, the Bible has not left open the prospect of collusion in regard to the resurrection narratives. Indeed, it cannot be denied (legitimately) that the resurrection accounts have come to us from independent sources. In his book, *Science vs. Religion*, Tad S. Clements vigorously denied that there is enough evidence to justify a personal belief in the resurrection. He did acknowledge, however: "There isn't merely one account of Christ's resurrection but rather an embarrassing multitude of stories..." (1990, p. 193). While he opined that these stories "disagree in significant respects," he nevertheless made it clear that the gospels are separate accounts of the same story. Dan Barker admitted the same when he boldly stated: "Since Easter [his term for the resurrection account—KB/EL] is told by five different writers, it gives one of the best chances to confirm or disconfirm the account" (1992, p. 179). One door that everyone on both sides of the resurrection controversy freely admits has been locked forever by the gospel accounts is the dead-bolted door against collusion.

DEALING WITH "CONTRADICTIONS"

Of course it will not be possible, in these few paragraphs, to deal with every alleged discrepancy between the resurrection accounts. But we would like to set forth some helpful principles that can be used to show that no genuine contradiction between the resurrection narratives has been documented.

Addition Does not a Contradiction Make

Suppose a man is telling a story about the time he and his wife went shopping at the mall. The man mentions all the great places in the mall to buy hunting supplies and cinnamon rolls. But the wife tells about the same shopping trip, yet mentions only the places to buy clothes. Is there a contradiction just because the wife mentioned only clothing stores, while the husband mentioned only cinnamon rolls and hunting supplies? No. They simply are adding to (or supplementing) each other's story to make it more complete. That same type of thing occurs quite frequently in the resurrection accounts.

As an example, Matthew's gospel account refers to "Mary Magdalene and the other Mary" as women who visited the tomb early on the first day of the week (Matthew 28:1). Mark cites Mary Magdalene, Mary the mother of James, and Salome as the callers (Mark 16:1). Luke mentions Mary Magdalene, Joanna, Mary the mother of James, and "the other women" (Luke 24:10). Yet John writes only about Mary Magdalene visiting Christ's tomb early on Sunday (John 20:1). Dan Barker cited these different names as discrepancies and/or contradictions (p. 182). But do these different lists truly contradict one another? No, they do not. They are supplementary (with each writer adding names to make the list more complete), but they are not contradictory. If John had said "**only** Mary Magdalene visited the tomb," or if Matthew had stated that "Mary Magdalene and the other Mary were the **only** women to visit the tomb," then there would be a contradiction. As it stands, however, no contradiction occurs. To further illustrate this point, suppose you have 10 one-dollar bills in your pocket. Someone comes up to you and asks, "Do you have a dollar bill in your pocket?" Naturally, you respond in the affirmative.

Suppose another person asks, "Do you have five dollars in your pocket?" and again you say that you do. Finally, another person asks, "Do you have ten dollars in your pocket?" and you say "yes" for the third time. Did you tell the truth every time? Yes, you did. Were all three statements about the contents of your pockets different? Yes, they were. But were any of your answers contradictory? No, they were not. How so? The fact is: supplementation does not equal contradiction!

Also relevant to this discussion about supplementation are the angels, men, and young man described in the different resurrection accounts. Two different "problems" arise with the entrance of the "holy heralds" at the empty tomb of Christ. First, exactly how many were there? Second, were they angels or men? The account in Matthew cites "an angel of the Lord who descended from heaven" and whose "appearance was as lightning, and his raiment white as snow" (28: 2-5). Mark's account presents a slightly different picture of "a young man sitting on the right side, arrayed in a white robe" (16:5). But Luke mentions that "two men stood by them [the women—KB/EL] in dazzling apparel" (24:4). And, finally, John writes about "two angels in white sitting, one at the head, and one at the feet, where the body of Jesus had lain" (20:12). Are any of these accounts contradictory as to the number of men or angels at the tomb? Factoring in the supplementation rule, we must answer in the negative. Although the accounts are different, they are not contradictory as to the number of messengers. Mark does not mention "**only** a young man" and Luke does not say there were "**exactly** two angels." Was there one messenger at the tomb? Yes, there was. Were there two as well? Yes, there were. Once again, note that supplementation does not equal contradiction.

Were They Men or Angels?

The second question concerning the messengers is their identity: Were they angels or men? Most people who are familiar with the Old Testament have no problem answering this question. Genesis chapters 18 and 19 mention three "men" who came to visit Abraham and Sarah. These men remained for a short time, and then two of them continued on to visit the city of Sodom. The Bible tells us in Genesis 19:1 that these "men" actually were angels. Yet when the men of Sodom came to do violence to these angels, the city dwellers asked: "Where are the men who came to you tonight?" (Genesis 19:5). Throughout the two chapters, the messengers are referred to both as men and as angels with equal accuracy. They looked, talked, walked, and sounded like men. Then could they be referred to (legitimately) as men? Yes. But were they in fact angels? Yes. Angels who appeared in human form.

To illustrate, suppose you saw a man sit down at a park bench and take off his right shoe. As you watched, he began to pull out an antenna from the toe of the shoe and a number pad from the heel. He proceeded to dial a number and began to talk to someone over his "shoe phone." If you were going to write down what you had seen, could you accurately say that the man dialed a number on his shoe? Yes. Could you also say that he dialed a number on his phone? Indeed, you could. The shoe had a heel, sole, toe, and everything else germane to a shoe, but in actuality it was much more than a shoe. In the same way, the messengers at the tomb could be described accurately as men. They had a head perched on two shoulders and held in place by a neck, and they had a body that was complete with arms and legs, etc. So, they were men. But, in truth, they were much more than men because they were angels—holy messengers sent from God's throne to deliver an announcement to certain people. Taking into account the fact that the Old Testament often uses the term "men" to describe angels who have assumed a human form, it is fairly easy to show that no contradiction exists concerning the identity of the messengers.

Perspective Plays a Part

What we continue to see in the independent resurrection narratives is not contradiction, but merely a difference in perspective. For instance, suppose a man had a 4x6 index card that was solid red on one side and solid white on the other. Further suppose that he stood in front of a large crowd, asked all the men to close their eyes, showed the women in the audience the red side of the card, and then had them scribble down what they saw. Further suppose that he had all the women close their eyes while he showed the men the white side of the card and had them write down what they saw. One group saw a red card and one group saw a white card. When their answers are compared, at first it would look like they were contradictory, yet they were not. The descriptions appeared contradictory because the two groups had a different perspective, since each had seen a different side of the same card. The perspective phenomenon plays a big part in everyday life. In the same way that no two witnesses ever see a car accident in exactly the same way, none of the witnesses of the resurrected Jesus saw the events from the same angle as the others.

Obviously, we have not dealt with every alleged discrepancy concerning the resurrection accounts. However, we have mentioned some of the major ones, which can be explained quite easily via the principles of supplementation or difference of perspective. An honest study of the remaining "problems" reveals that not a single legitimate contradiction exists between the narratives; they may be **different** in some aspects, but they are **not contradictory**. Furthermore, whatever differences do exist prove that no collusion took place and document the diversity that would be expected from different individuals witnessing the same event.

The Problem with Miracles

Based on historical grounds, the resurrection of Jesus Christ has as much or more evidence to verify its credibility than any other event in ancient history. Unfortunately, this evidence often gets tossed aside by those who deny the possibility of miracles.

But when it comes to Christ's resurrection, some prefer to use a strictly empirical approach, and as a result, have decided what is, and what is not, possible in **their** world. And miracles (like the resurrection) do not fall into their "possible" category. Since they never have seen anyone raised from the dead, and since no scientific experiments can be performed on a resurrected body, they then assume that the gospel resurrection accounts must have some natural explanation(s). In an article titled, "Why I Don't Buy the Resurrection," Richard Carrier embodied the gist of this argument in the following comment:

> No amount of argument can convince me to trust a 2000-year-old second-hand report over what I see, myself, directly, here and now, with my own eyes. If I observe facts which entail that I will cease to exist when I die, then the Jesus story can never override that observation, being infinitely weaker as a proof. And yet all the evidence before my senses confirms my mortality.... A 2000-year-old second-hand tale from the backwaters of an illiterate and ignorant land can never overpower these facts. I see no one returning to life after their brain has completely died from lack of oxygen. I have had no conversations with spirits of the dead. What I see is quite the opposite of everything this tall tale claims. How can it command more respect than my own two eyes? It cannot (2000).

Although such an argument at first may appear perfectly plausible, it encounters two insurmountable difficulties. First, there are things that took place in the past that no one alive today has seen or ever will see, yet they still are accepted as fact. The origin of life on this planet provides a good example. Regardless of whether a person believes in creation or evolution, he or she must admit that some things happened in the past that are not still occurring today (or at least that have not been witnessed). To evolutionists, we pose the question: "Have you ever personally used your five senses to establish that a nonliving thing can give rise to a living thing." Of course, evolutionists must admit that they never have seen such happen, in spite of all the origin-of-life experiments that have been performed over the last fifty years. Does such an admission mean, then, that evolutionists do not accept the idea that life came from nonliving matter, just because they never have witnessed such an event? Of course not. Instead, we are asked to consider "ancient evidence" (like the geologic column and the fossil record) that evolutionists believe leads to such a conclusion. Still, the hard fact remains that no one alive today (or, for that matter, anyone who ever lived in the past) has witnessed something living come from something nonliving by natural processes.

Following this same line of reasoning, those who believe in creation freely admit that the creation of life on Earth is an event that has not been witnessed by anyone alive today (or, for that matter, anyone else in the past, except possibly Adam). It was a unique, one-time-only event that cannot be duplicated by experiment and cannot currently be detected by the five human senses. As with evolutionists, creationists ask us to examine evidence such as the fossil record, the inherent design of the Universe and its inhabitants, the Law of Cause and Effect, the Law of Biogenesis, etc., which they believe leads to the conclusion that life was created at some point in the past by an intelligent Creator. But, before we drift too far from our primary topic of the resurrection, remember that this brief discussion concerning creation and evolution is inserted only to establish one point—everyone must admit that he or she accepts some concepts from the distant past without having personally inspected them using the empirical senses.

Second, it is true that a dead person rising from the dead would be an amazing and, yes, empirically astonishing event. People do not normally rise from the dead in the everyday scheme of things. Yet, was not that the very point the apostles and other witnesses of the resurrection were trying to get people to understand? If Jesus of Nazareth truly rose from the grave never to die again—thereby accomplishing something that no mortal man ever had accomplished—would not that be enough to prove that He was the Son of God as He had claimed (see Mark 14:61-62)? He had predicted that He would be raised from the dead (John 2:19). And He was!

Those first-century onlookers certainly understood that a person rising from the dead was not natural, because even they understood how the laws of nature worked. As C.S. Lewis explained:

> But there is one thing often said about our ancestors which we must not say. We must not say "They believed in miracles because they did not know the Laws of Nature." This is nonsense. When St. Joseph discovered that his bride was pregnant, he "was minded to put her away." He knew enough about biology for that.... When the disciples saw Christ walking on the water they were frightened; they would not have been frightened unless they had known the Laws of Nature and known that this was an exception (1970, p. 26).

The apostle Paul underscored this point in Romans 1:4 when he stated that Jesus Christ was "declared to be the Son of God with power, according to the spirit of holiness, by the resurrection from the dead." The entire point of Christ's resurrection was, and is, that it proved His deity. As we stated earlier, most people who deny the resurrection do so because they refuse to believe in a God Who performs miracles, not because the historical evidence is insufficient.

Face the Facts

When dealing with the resurrection of Christ, we must concentrate on the facts. Jesus of Nazareth lived. He died. His tomb was empty. The apostles preached that they saw Him after He physically rose from the dead. The apostles suffered and died because they preached, and refused to deny, the resurrection. Their message is preserved in the most accurate document of which ancient history can boast. Independent witnesses addressed the resurrection in their writings—with enough diversity (yet without a single legitimate contradiction) to prove that no collusion took place.

The primary argument against the resurrection, of course, is that during the normal course of events, dead people do not rise from the grave—which was the very point being made by the apostles. But when all the evidence is weighed and it is revealed that the apostles never buckled under torture, the New Testament never crumples under scrutiny, and the secular, historical witnesses refuse to be drowned in a sea of criticism, then it is evident that the resurrection of Jesus Christ demands its rightful place in the annals of history as the most important event this world has ever seen. To quote the immortal words of the Holy Spirit as spoken through the apostle Paul to King Agrippa in the great long ago: "Why should it be thought incredible by you that God raises the dead?" (Acts 26:8).

WHAT'S SO IMPORTANT ABOUT JESUS' RESURRECTION?

After the widow's son died, Elijah prayed to God, "and the soul of the child came back to him, and he revived" (1 Kings 17:22). A few years later, the prophet Elisha raised the dead son of a Shunammite (2 Kings 4:32-35). Then, after Elisha's death, a dead man, in the process of being buried in the tomb of Elisha, was restored to life after touching Elisha's bones (2 Kings 13:20-21). When Jesus was on Earth, He raised the daughter of Jairus from the dead (Mark 8:21-24,35-43), as well as the widow of Nain's son (Luke 7:11-16), and Lazarus, whose body had been buried for four days (John 11:1-45). After Jesus' death and resurrection, Matthew recorded how "the graves were opened; and many bodies of the saints who had fallen asleep were raised; and coming out of the graves after His resurrection, they went into the holy city and appeared to many" (27:52-53). Then later, during the early years of the church, Peter raised Tabitha from the dead (Acts 9:36-43), while Paul raised the young man Eutychus, who had died after falling out of a three-story window (Acts 20:7-12). All of these people died, and later rose to live again. Although some of the individuals arose very shortly after death, Lazarus and (most likely) the saints who were raised after the resurrection of Jesus, were entombed longer than was Jesus. In view of all of these resurrections, some have asked, "What is so important about Jesus' resurrection?" If others in the past have died to live again, what makes His resurrection so special? Why is the resurrection of Jesus more significant than any other?

First, similar to how the miracles of Jesus were performed in order to set Him apart as the Son of God and the promised Messiah, even though all others who worked miracles during Bible times were not God in the flesh, the miracles of Jesus are more significant than other miracles simply because the inspired apostles and prophets said that they were. Many people throughout the Bible worked miracles in order to confirm their divine message (cf. Mark 16:20; Hebrews 2:1-4), but only Jesus did them as proof of His divine **nature**. Once, during the Feast of Dedication in Jerusalem, a group of Jews surrounded Jesus and asked, "If You are the Christ, tell us plainly" (John 10:24)? Jesus responded to them saying, "I told you, and you do not believe. The works that I do in My Father's name, they bear witness of Me.... I and My Father are one" (John 10:25,30). These Jews understood that Jesus claimed to be the Son of God in the flesh (cf. 10: 33,36), and Jesus wanted them to understand that this truth could be known as a result of the miracles that He worked, which testified of His deity (cf. John 20: 30-31). Why? **Because He said they did** (10:25,35-38; cf. John 5:36). The miracles that Jesus performed bore witness of the fact that He was from the Father (John 5:36), **because He said He was from the Father**. A miracle in and of itself did not mean the person who worked it was deity. Moses, Elijah, Elisha, Peter, Paul, and a host of others worked miracles, with some even raising people from the dead, but not for the purpose of proving they were God in the flesh. The apostles and prophets of the New Testament worked miracles to confirm their message that Jesus was the Son of God, not to prove that they were God (cf. Acts 14:8-18).

Jesus, on the other hand, performed miracles to bear witness that He was the Son of God, just as He claimed to be (cf. John 9:35-38).

Likewise, one reason that Jesus' miraculous **resurrection** is more significant than the resurrections of Lazarus, Tabitha, Eutychus, or anyone else who was raised from the dead, is simply because the inspired apostles and prophets in the early church said that it was more important. Like the miracles He worked during His earthly ministry that testified of His deity, His resurrection also bore witness of His divine nature. There is no record of anyone alleging that Lazarus was God's Son based upon his resurrection, nor did the early church claim divinity for Eutychus or Tabitha because they died and came back to life. None of the above-mentioned individuals who were resurrected ever claimed that their resurrection was proof of deity, nor did any inspired prophet or apostle. On the other hand, Jesus was "declared to be the Son of God with power...by the resurrection from the dead" (Romans 1:4). His resurrection was different because of Who He was—the Son of God. Just as the miracles He worked during His earthly ministry testified of His divine message, and thus also of His divine nature, so did His resurrection.

Second, the significance of Jesus' resurrection is seen in the fact that He was the first to rise from the dead **never to die again**. Since no one who has risen from the dead is still living on Earth, and since there is no evidence in the Bible that God ever took someone who had risen from the dead into heaven without dying again, it is reasonable to conclude that all who have ever risen from the dead, died in later years.

Jesus, however, "having been raised from the dead, dies no more. Death no longer has dominion over Him" (Romans 6:9). Jesus said of Himself: "I am the First and the Last. I am He who lives, and was dead, and behold, I am alive forevermore" (Revelation 1: 17-18). All others who previously were raised at one time, died again, and are among those who "sleep" and continue to wait for the bodily resurrection. Only Jesus has truly **conquered** death. Only His bodily resurrection was followed by eternal life, rather than another physical death. Although it has been argued by skeptics that "it's the Resurrection, per se, that matters, not the fact that Jesus never died again" (see McKinsey, 1983, p. 1), Paul actually linked the two together, saying, God "raised Him from the dead, **no more to return to corruption**" (Acts 13:34, emp. added). Furthermore, the writer of Hebrews argued for a better life through Jesus on the basis of His termination of death. One reason for the inadequacy of the old priesthood was because "they were prevented by death." Jesus, however, because He rose never to die again, "continues forever" in "an unchangeable priesthood," and lives to make intercession for His people (Hebrews 7: 23-25).

A third reason why Jesus' resurrection stands out above all others is because it alone was foretold in the Old Testament. In his sermon on the Day of Pentecost, Peter affirmed that God had raised Jesus from the dead because it was not possible for the grave to hold Him. As proof, he quoted Psalm 16:8-11.

> I foresaw the Lord always before my face, for He is at my right hand, that I may not be shaken. Therefore my heart rejoiced, and my tongue was

> glad; moreover my flesh also will rest in hope. For You will not leave my soul in Hades, nor will You allow Your Holy One to see corruption. You have made known to me the ways of life; You will make me full of joy in Your presence (Acts 2:25-28).

Peter then explained this quote from Psalms by saying:

> Men and brethren, let me speak freely to you of the patriarch David, that he is both dead and buried, and his tomb is with us to this day. Therefore, being a prophet, and knowing that God had sworn with an oath to him that of the fruit of his body, according to the flesh, He would raise up the Christ to sit on his throne, he, foreseeing this, spoke concerning the resurrection of the Christ, that His soul was not left in Hades, nor did His flesh see corruption. This Jesus God has raised up, of which we are all witnesses (Acts 2:29-32).

The apostle Paul also believed that the psalmist bore witness to Christ, and spoke of His resurrection. In his address at Antioch of Pisidia, he said:

> And we declare to you glad tidings—that promise which was made to the fathers. God has fulfilled this for us their children, in that He has raised up Jesus. As it is also written in the second Psalm: "You are My Son, today I have begotten You." And that He raised Him from the dead, no more to return to corruption, He has spoken thus: "I will give you the sure mercies of David." Therefore He also says in another Psalm: "You will not allow Your Holy One to see corruption." For David, after he had served his own generation by the will of God, fell asleep, was buried with his fathers, and saw corruption; but

> He whom God raised up saw no corruption. Therefore let it be known to you, brethren, that through this Man is preached to you the forgiveness of sins; and by Him everyone who believes is justified from all things from which you could not be justified by the law of Moses (Acts 13:32-39).

Where is the prophecy for the resurrection of Jairus' daughter? When did the prophets ever foretell of Eutychus or Tabitha's resurrection? Such instances are not found within Scripture. No resurrected person other than Jesus had his or her resurrection foretold by an Old Testament prophet. This certainly makes Jesus' resurrection unique.

Fourth, the significance of Jesus' resurrection is seen in the fact that His resurrection was preceded by numerous instances in which He prophesied that He would defeat death, even foretelling the exact day on which it would occur. Jesus told some scribes and Pharisees on one occasion, "For as Jonah was three days and three nights in the belly of the great fish, **so will the Son of Man be three days and three nights in the heart of the earth**" (Matthew 12:40, emp. added). Matthew, Mark, and Luke all recorded how Jesus "began to show to His disciples that He must go to Jerusalem, and suffer many things from the elders and chief priests and scribes, and be killed, and **be raised the third day**" (Matthew 16:21, emp. added; cf. Mark 8:31-32; Luke 9:22). While Jesus and His disciples were in Galilee, Jesus reminded them, saying, "The Son of Man is about to be betrayed into the hands of men, and they will kill Him, and **the third day He will be raised up**" (Matthew 17:22-23, emp. added). Just before His triumphal entry into Jerusalem, Jesus again reminded His disciples, saying, "Behold, we are going up to Jerusalem, and the Son of Man will be betrayed to the chief priests and to the scribes; and they will condemn Him to death, and deliver Him to the Gentiles to mock and to scourge and to crucify. **And the third day He will rise again**" (Matthew 20:18-19, emp. added). Jesus' prophecies concerning His resurrection and the specific day on which it would occur were so widely known that, after Jesus' death, His enemies requested that Pilate place a guard at the tomb, saying, "Sir, we remember, while He was still alive, how that deceiver said, 'After three days I will rise.' Therefore command that the tomb be made secure **until the third day**..." (Matthew 27:63-64, emp. added). They knew exactly what Jesus had said He would do, and they did everything in their power to stop it.

Where are the prophecies from the son of the widow from Zarephath? Had he prophesied of his resurrection prior to his death? Or what about the son of the Shunammite woman whom Elisha raised from the dead? Where are his personal prophecies? Truly, no one mentioned in the Bible who rose from the dead prophesied about his or her resurrection beforehand, other than Jesus. And certainly no one ever prophesied about the exact day on which he or she would arise from the dead, save Jesus. This prior knowledge and prophecy makes His resurrection a significant event. He overcame death, just as He predicted. He did **exactly** what he said He was going to do, on the **exact** day He said He was going to do it.

Finally, the uniqueness of Jesus' resurrection is seen in the fact that He is the only resurrected person ever to have lived and died without having committed one sin during His lifetime. He was "pure" and "righteous" (1 John 3:3; 2:1), "Who committed no sin, nor was deceit found in His mouth" (1 Peter 2:22). He was "a lamb without blemish and without spot" (1 Peter 1:19), "Who knew no sin" (2 Corinthians 5:21). No one else who has risen from the dead ever lived a perfect life, and then died prior to his or her resurrection for the purpose of taking away the sins of the world (cf. John 1:29). Because Jesus lived a sinless life, died, and then overcame death in His resurrection, He alone has the honor of being called "the Lamb of God" and the "great High Priest" (Hebrews 4:14). "Christ was offered once to bear the sins of many," and because of His resurrection "those who eagerly wait for Him He will appear a second time, apart from sin, for salvation" (Hebrews 9:28).

Whether or not Eutychus, Tabitha, Lazarus, etc., rose from the grave, our relationship with God is not affected. Without Jesus' resurrection, however, there would be no "Prince and Savior, to give repentance to Israel and forgiveness of sins" (Acts 5:31). Without Jesus' resurrection, He would not be able to make intercession for us (Hebrews 7:25). Without Jesus' resurrection, we would have no assurance of His coming and subsequent judgment (Acts 17:31).

Most certainly, Jesus' resurrection is significant—more so than any other resurrection ever to have taken place. Only Jesus' resurrection was verbalized by inspired men as proof of His deity. Only Jesus rose never to die again. Only Jesus' resurrection was prophesied in the Old Testament. Only Jesus prophesied of the precise day in which He would rise from the grave, and then fulfilled that prediction. Only Jesus' resurrection was preceded by a perfect life—a life lived, given up, and restored in the resurrection for the purpose of becoming man's Prince, Savior, and Mediator.

CHAPTER 7

ANSWERING ATTACKS UPON THE DEITY OF CHRIST

Once skeptics come to the realization that the evidence for the historicity of Christ and the historical accuracy of the New Testament cannot logically be explained away, the next step frequently taken by critics of Christ is to attack the Bible's own portrayal of Jesus. If the enemies of Christ can discredit His claims of divinity by demonstrating that He either did not fulfill Old Testament prophecies or that the New Testament reveals instances of deceitfulness and inappropriate behavior in His life, then Jesus certainly could not be Who He and the Bible writers claimed that He was—God in the flesh (John 1:1,14). But, if the charges against Jesus' life and character are proven to be fallacious or unsubstantiated, then such accusations should be dismissed, and Jesus' true identity must either be accepted or rejected based upon the fact that the Bible's portrayal of the life of Christ is consistent with His claims of deity.

"He Opened Not His Mouth"

In what many consider to be the most well-known prophecy concerning the coming of the Messiah, the prophet Isaiah foretold of the sufferings that Christ would endure amid His trial and crucifixion, saying (as if it had already happened):

> But He was wounded for our transgressions, He was bruised for our iniquities; the chastisement for our peace was upon Him, and by His stripes we are healed.... He was oppressed and He was afflicted, **yet He opened not His mouth**; He was led as a lamb to the slaughter, and as a sheep before its shearers is silent, **so He opened not His mouth** (53:5,7, emp. added).

According to Isaiah, not only was the Messiah going to suffer cruel punishment on His way to the grave, but He would do so without opening His mouth. He would be as silent as a sheep is before its shearers.

The problem that some have with this passage is that the gospel writers indicate that Jesus **did** open His mouth before His accusers, and also later while hanging on the cross. After Jesus was arrested in the Garden of Gethsemane, the high priest questioned Jesus, saying, "Are You the Christ, the Son of the Blessed?" Jesus responded, not with silence, but with two statements that infuriated the Jewish council. He said: "I am. And you will see the Son of Man sitting at the right hand of the Power, and coming with the clouds of heaven" (Mark 14:61-62). Jesus was then sent to Pilate where He was asked another question about His identity, "Are You the King of the Jews?" As He had done earlier that night, He did not keep silent, but answered Pilate with these words: "It is as you say" (Mark 15:2). Even while hanging on the cross a few hours later, Jesus made several statements, including, "Father, forgive them, for they do not know what they do" (Luke 23:34) and "My God, My God, why have You forsaken Me?" (Mark 15:34). So how could the suffering servant of Isaiah 53 be referring to Jesus, since He did, in fact, "open His mouth," both during His trial, and while hanging on the cross?

Obviously, if the phrase, "He opened not His mouth," meant that the Messiah would never speak one word while being oppressed and afflicted, then Jesus could not have been the prophesied suffering servant, and the inspired writers, preachers, and prophets of the first century who applied this passage to Him were mistaken (cf. Acts 8:32-33). A proper understanding of this phrase, however, reveals that it does not literally mean the accused "did not open his mouth." First, not even the skeptic would interpret this verse to mean that the suffering servant literally kept his mouth closed—that if he ever separated his lips so as to allow air, water, or food to enter his mouth, then the prophecy would be annulled. Such would be a ridiculous interpretation of the phrase "he opened not his mouth," because in this passage Isaiah clearly used the word "mouth" to refer to what the mouth **does**—it aids in speaking—a figure of speech known as metonymy (of the cause). Second, the phrases "open the mouth" and "do not open the mouth" are Hebrew idioms (appearing both in the Old and the New Testaments), which frequently are used to refer more to the length, freedom, and/or kind of speech, rather than whether one or more words actually are (or are not) spoken.

When Jephthah (the ninth judge of Israel listed in the book of Judges) spoke to his daughter following the victory that the Lord had given Israel over the Ammonites, He said: "Alas, my daughter! You have brought me very low! You are among those who trouble me! For **I have given my word to the Lord,** and I cannot go back on it" (Judges 11:35, emp. added). The phrase "I have given my word to the Lord" in the New King James Version is literally, "I have **opened my mouth** unto the Lord" (KJV, emp. added; see ASV). Jephthah had earlier made a vow to the Lord, saying, "If You will indeed deliver the people of Ammon into my hands, then it will be that whatever comes out of the doors of my house to meet me, when I return in peace of Ammon, shall surely be the Lord's and I will offer it up as a burnt offering" (Judges 11:30-31). The reason that Jephthah was so distraught after returning home from war and seeing his daughter was not simply because he "opened his mouth" and prayed to God, but because included in this prayer was a **promise** to God—one that caused himself and his daughter great sadness. Jephthah could have spoken to God all day without making such a significant and life-changing statement, and it not have been described as a time in which Jephthah "opened his mouth." The phrase "opened my (thy) mouth" (Judges 11:35,36) meant that something extremely noteworthy was stated; a promise to God was made that could not be broken.

Notice also how the idea of "opening one's mouth" is used on occasion in the New Testament. Sometime after Philip had spoken with the eunuch from Ethiopia about the passage of Scripture from which he was reading (Isaiah 53 ironically enough—see Acts 8:30-33), the text states: "Then Philip **opened his mouth**, and beginning at this Scripture, preached Jesus to Him" (Acts 8:35, emp. added). Notice that Philip already had been speaking with the eunuch (8:30), and most likely had made other introductory comments to this stranger that are not recorded by Luke in the book of

Acts. However, it was not until Philip began to speak **at length** to the eunuch, and to **preach to him** the good news of Jesus, that Philip was described as one who "opened his mouth."

In chapter ten of the book of Acts, Luke recorded Peter's visit with a Gentile named Cornelius. After being summoned by the Spirit of God (10:19-20) to travel to the city of Cornelius (i.e., Caesarea), Peter departed on the next day. Upon his arrival, Peter spoke to Cornelius about several things (Acts 10:25-29). He first rebuked Cornelius for worshiping him, saying, "Stand up; I myself am also a man" (10:26). He proceeded to speak with him about other things not specifically mentioned in the text (10:27). And then he revealed to Cornelius and his household that God had shown him (a Jew) that Gentiles should no longer be considered unclean. After several minutes (or perhaps even a few hours) of conversation between Peter and Cornelius (10:24-33), Luke then recorded that "Peter **opened his mouth**" (10:34) and gave a defense of the Christ and the Christian faith. Had Peter's mouth been "open" before this time? Yes. Had he already **spoken** to Cornelius about several things? Certainly. Now Peter **really** begins to speak. He had already been speaking, but now he "opens his mouth." Now he **preaches** the Gospel of Christ.

In writing to the church at Corinth, Paul once made the comment: "Our **mouth is open** unto you, O Corinthians" (2 Corinthians 6:11, ASV, emp. added). This statement obviously carries more meaning than simply, "Paul **spoke** to the Corinthians." Certain modern versions translate this verse using such words as "openly" (NKJV) or "freely" (NIV) to describe how Paul and Timothy spoke to the Corinthians. Rather than suppressing various truths that would be beneficial to the church at Corinth (cf. 2 Corinthians 4:2-3), they spoke openly and without restraint. They **unreservedly** commended themselves and their ministry to the Corinthians in order that they might accept their message (cf. 2 Corinthians 6:1-2; see Jamieson, et al., 1997). This is how Paul used the phrase "to open the mouth."

When the prophet Isaiah wrote that the suffering Servant "opened **not** His mouth" while being oppressed and afflicted (Isaiah 53:7), he did not mean that Jesus never uttered a word from the time He was arrested in the garden until His death on the cross. The thought behind this phrase is that Jesus would not speak **freely** and **unreservedly** in defense of Himself. Whereas Jesus could have responded to His accusers with "an open mouth" by giving a strong, lengthy defense of His innocence (similar to how Philip, Peter, and Paul testified of both Christ and their own ministry with "an open mouth"), Jesus chose to restrain Himself before His accusers and tormentors. Rather than calling twelve legions of angels to fight this battle for Him (cf. Matthew 26:53), Jesus humbly submitted to His enemies. Rather than performing some notable miracle before Herod so as to gain His freedom (cf. Luke 23:8), and instead of striking the high priest with blindness in an attempt to convince the Sanhredrin that He truly was the Son of God, Jesus suppressed His powers. Less than twenty-four hours earlier, Jesus had healed Malchus' severed ear, yet Jesus did nothing to lighten His **own** affliction during His trial and crucifixion—not even mentioning this miracle so as to defend His deity. In light of what Christ **could** have done to His accusers and what oral defense He **could** have given before them on His own behalf, Christ's passive submission before them is remarkable. Truly, "[w]hen He was reviled, did not revile in return; when He suffered, He did not threaten, but committed Himself to Him who judges righteously" (1 Peter 2:23).

To prophesy that the Suffering Servant "opened not His mouth," is to use a hyperbolic expression which means that Jesus refrained from giving an exhaustive legal defense on His own behalf. During much of His affliction and oppression He was completely silent (cf. Matthew 26:62-63; 27:12-14). At other times He spoke only a few words—none of which came close to being the kind of defense He could have offered on His own behalf had He been trying to avoid persecution and crucifixion.

Was Jesus Trustworthy?

When Christ spoke to a group of hostile Jews in Jerusalem regarding God the Father, and His own equality with Him (John 5:17-30; cf. 10:30), He defended His deity by pointing to several witnesses, including John the Baptizer, the Father in heaven, and the Scriptures (5:33-47). One statement that has confused some Bible readers concerning Jesus' defense of His deity is found in John 5:31. Jesus began this part of His discourse by saying, "If I bear witness of Myself, **My witness is not true**" (emp. added). According to many Bible critics, this declaration blatantly contradicts the following statement He made on another occasion when speaking to the Pharisees. He said: "Even if I bear witness of Myself, **My witness is true**" (John 8:14, emp. added). How could He say that His witness was both true, and not true, without having lied?

Consider the following illustration. An innocent man on trial for murder is judged to be guilty by the jury, even after proclaiming his innocence. (Someone had framed the defendant for the murder, and all the evidence the jury heard pointed to the defendant as the offender.) When leaving the court house, if the man who was wrongly convicted is asked by a reporter, "Are you guilty?," and he responds by saying, "If the court says I'm guilty, I'm guilty," has the man lied? Even though the statements, "I am guilty," and "I am not guilty," are totally different, they may not be contradictory, depending on the time and sense in which they are spoken. After the trial, the wrongly accused defendant simply repeated the jury's verdict. He said, "I am guilty," and meant, "The court has found me guilty."

When Jesus conceded to the Jews the fact that His witness was "not true," He was not confessing to being a liar. Rather, Jesus was reacting to a well-known law of His day. In Greek, Roman, and Jewish law, the testimony of a witness could not be received in his own case (Robertson, 1997). "Witness to anyone must always be borne by someone else" (Morris, 1995, p. 287). The Law of Moses stated: "One witness shall not rise against a man concerning any iniquity or any sin that he commits; by the mouth of two or three witnesses the matter shall be established" (Deuteronomy 19:15; cf. Matthew 18:15-17). The Pharisees understood this law well, as is evident by their statement to Jesus: "You bear witness of Yourself; Your witness is not true" (John 8:13). In John 5:31, "Jesus points to the impossibility of anyone's being accepted on the basis of his own word.... He is asserting that if of himself he were to bear witness to himself, that would make it untrue" in a court of law (Morris, p. 287). If Jesus had no evidence in a trial regarding His deity other than His own testimony about Himself, His testimony would be inconclusive and inadmissible. Jesus understood that His audience had a right to expect more evidence than just His word. Similar to the above illustration where an innocent man accepts the guilty verdict of the jury as final, Jesus said, "My witness is not true," and meant that, **in accordance with the law**, His own testimony apart from other witnesses would be considered invalid (or insufficient to establish truth).

But why is it that Jesus said to the Pharisees at a later time that His "witness **is** true" (John 8:14)? The difference is that, in this instance, Jesus was stressing the fact that **His words** were true. Even if in a court of law two witnesses are required for a fact to be established (a law Jesus enunciated in verse 17), that law does not take away the fact that Jesus was telling the truth, just as it did not take away the fact that the wrongly accused man mentioned above was telling the truth during his trial. Jesus declared His testimony to be true for the simple reason that His testimony revealed the true facts regarding Himself (Lenski, 1961b, p. 599). He then followed this pronouncement of truth with the fact that there was another witness—the Father in heaven Who sent Him to Earth (8:16-18). Thus, in actuality, His testimony was true in two senses: (1) it was true because it was indeed factual; and (2) it was valid because it was corroborated by a second unimpeachable witness—the Father.

God the Father (John 8:18; 5:37-38), along with John the Baptizer (John 5:33), the miraculous signs of Jesus (5:36), the Scriptures (5:39), and specifically the writings of Moses (5:46), all authenticated the true statements Jesus made regarding His deity. Sadly, many of His listeners rejected the evidence then, just as people reject it today.

Did Jesus Ignore the Fourth Commandment?

Like many critics of the life of Christ today, the first-century Pharisees certainly did not think that the Son of God was beyond reproach. Following Jesus' feeding of the four thousand, the Pharisees came "testing" Him, asking Him to show them a sign from heaven (Matthew 16:1). Later in the book of Matthew (19: 3ff.), the writer recorded how "the Pharisees also came to Him, **testing Him**, and saying to Him, 'Is it lawful for a man to divorce his wife for just any reason?' " It was their aim on this occasion, as on numerous other occasions, to entangle Jesus in His teachings by asking Him a potentially entrapping question—one that, if answered in a way that the Pharisees had anticipated, might bring upon Jesus the wrath of Herod Antipas (cf. Matthew 14:1-12; Mark 6:14-29) and/or some of His fellow Jews (e.g., the school of Hillel, or the school of Shammai). A third time the Pharisees sought to "entangle Him in His talk" (Matthew 22:15) as they asked, "Is it lawful to pay taxes to Caesar, or not?" (22: 17). The jealous and hypocritical Pharisees were so relentless in their efforts to destroy the Lord's influence, that on one occasion they even accused Jesus' disciples of breaking the law as they "went through the grainfields on the Sabbath...were hungry, and began to pluck heads of grain and to eat" (Matthew 12: 1ff.). [NOTE: "Their knowledge of so trifling an incident shows how minutely they observed all his deeds" (Coffman, 1984, p. 165). The microscopic scrutiny under which Jesus lived likely was even more relentless than what some "stars" experience today. In one sense, the Pharisees could be considered the "paparazzi" of Jesus' day.] Allegedly, what Jesus allowed His disciples to do on this particular Sabbath was considered "work," which the Law of Moses forbade (Matthew 12:2; cf. Exodus 20:9-10; 34:21).

Jesus responded to the criticism of the Pharisees by giving the truth of the matter, and at the same time revealing the Pharisees' hypocrisy. As was somewhat customary for Jesus when being tested by His enemies (cf. Matthew 12:11-12; 15:3; 21:24-25; etc.), He responded to the Pharisees' accusation with two questions. First, He asked: "Have you not read what David did when he was hungry, he and those who were with him: how he entered the house of God and ate the showbread which was not lawful for him to eat, nor for those who were with him, but only for the priests?" (12:3-4). Jesus reminded the Pharisees of an event in the life of David (recorded in 1 Samuel 21:1ff.), where he and others, while fleeing from king Saul, ate of the showbread, which divine law restricted to the priests (Leviticus 24:5-9). Some commentators have unjustifiably concluded that Jesus was implying innocence on the part of David (and that God's laws are subservient to human needs—cf. Zerr, 1952, 5:41; Dummelow, 1937, p. 666), and thus He was defending His disciples "lawless" actions with the same reasoning. Actually, however, just the opposite is true. Jesus explicitly stated that what David did was wrong ("not lawful"—12:4), and that what His disciples did was right—they were "guiltless" (12:7). Furthermore, as J.W. McGarvey observed: "If Christians may violate law when its observance would involve hardship or suffering, then there is an end to suffering for the name of Christ, and an end even of self-denial" (1875, p. 104). The disciples were not permitted by Jesus to break the law on this occasion (or any other) just because it was inconvenient (cf. Matthew 5:17-19). The Pharisees simply were wrong in their accusations. Like many of Jesus' enemies today, "The Pharisees were out to 'get' Jesus; and any charge was better than none" (Coffman, 1984, p. 165). The only "law" Jesus' disciples broke was the pharisaical interpretation of the law (which was more sacred to some Pharisees than the law itself). In response to such hyper-legalism, Burton Coffman forcefully stated: "In the Pharisees' view, the disciples were guilty of threshing wheat! **Such pedantry, nit-picking, and magnification of trifles would also have made them guilty of irrigating land, if they had chanced to knock off a few drops of dew while passing through the fields**!" (p. 165, emp. added).

Jesus used the instruction of 1 Samuel 21 to cause the Pharisees to recognize their insincerity, and to exonerate His disciples. David, a man about whom the Jews ever boasted, blatantly violated God's law by eating the showbread, and yet the Pharisees justified him. On the other hand, Jesus' disciples merely plucked some grain on the Sabbath while walking through a field—an act that the law permitted—yet the Pharisees condemned them. Had the Pharisees not approved of David's conduct, they could have responded by saying, "You judge yourself. You're all sinners." Their reaction to Jesus' question—silence—was that of hypocrites who had been exposed.

Jesus then asked a second question, saying, "Have you not read in the law that on the Sabbath the priests in the temple profane the Sabbath, and are blameless?" (Matthew 12:5). Here, Jesus wanted the Pharisees to acknowledge that even the law itself condoned **some** work on the Sabbath day. Although the Pharisees acted as if **all** work was banned on this day, it was actually the busiest day of the week for priests.

> They baked and changed the showbread; they performed sabbatical sacrifices (Num. xxviii. 9), and two lambs were killed on the sabbath in addition to the daily sacrifice. This involved the killing, skinning, and cleaning of the animals, and the building of the fire to consume the sacrifice. They also trimmed the gold lamps, burned incense, and performed various other duties (McGarvey, n.d., *The Fourfold...*, pp. 211-212).

One of those "other duties" would have been to circumcise young baby boys when the child's eighth day fell on a Sabbath (Leviticus 12:3; John 7:22-23). The purpose of Jesus citing these "profane" priestly works was to prove that the Sabbath prohibition was not unconditional. [NOTE: Jesus used the term "profane," not because there was a real desecration of the temple by the priests as they worked, but "to express what was true according to the mistaken notions of the Pharisees as to manual works performed on the Sabbath" (Bullinger, 1898, p. 676).] The truth is, the Sabbath law "did not forbid work absolutely, but labor for worldly gain. Activity in the work of God was both allowed and commanded" (McGarvey, n.d., *The Four-*

fold..., p. 212). Coffman thus concluded: "Just as the priests served the temple on the Sabbath day and were guiltless, his [Jesus'—KB/EL] disciples might also serve Christ, the Greater Temple, without incurring guilt" (1984, p. 167). Just as the priests who served God in the temple on the Sabbath were totally within the law, so likewise were Jesus' disciples as they served the "Lord of the Sabbath" (Matthew 12:8), Whose holiness was greater than that of the temple (12:6).

Did Jesus Break the Fifth Commandment?

Consider the mother who asks her son to do something for a neighbor, and the son responds to his mother by saying, "**Woman**, what does that have to do with me?" Responding to a mother's (or any woman's) request in twenty-first-century America with the refrain, "Woman...," sounds impolite and offensive. Furthermore, a Christian, who is commanded to honor his father and mother (Ephesians 6:2), would be out of line in most situations when using such an expression while talking directly to His mother.

In light of the ill-mannered use of the word "woman" in certain contexts today, some question how Jesus could have spoken to His mother 2,000 years ago using this term without breaking the commandment to "[h]onor your father and your mother" (Exodus 20:12; cf. Matthew 15:4; Matthew 5:17-20). When Jesus, His disciples, and His mother were at the wedding in Cana of Galilee where there was a depletion of wine, Mary said to Jesus, "They have no wine" (John 2:3). Jesus then responded to his mother, saying, "Woman, what does your concern have to do with Me? My hour has not yet come" (John 2:4). Notice what one skeptic has written regarding what Jesus said in this verse.

> In Matt. 15:4 he [Jesus—KB/EL] told people to "Honor thy father and thy mother"; yet, he was one of the first to ignore his own maxim by saying to his mother in John 4:24, "Woman, what have I to do with thee?" (McKinsey, 1995, p. 44).
>
> Imagine someone talking to his own mother in such a disrespectful manner and addressing her by such an impersonal noun as 'woman.' Talk about an insolent offspring! (p. 134).
>
> Jesus needs to practice some parental respect... (McKinsey, 2000, p. 251).
>
> Apparently Jesus' love escaped him (McKinsey, n.d., "Jesus...").
>
> Why was Jesus disrespectful of his mother? In John 2:4, Jesus uses the same words with his mother that demons use when they meet Jesus. Surely the son of God knew that Mary had the blessing of the Father, didn't he, (and she was the mother of God—Ed.) not to mention the fact that the son of God would never be rude? (McKinsey, n.d., "Problems...," parenthetical comment in orig.).

As one can see, Mr. McKinsey is adamant that Jesus erred. He used such words to describe Jesus as disrespectful, insolent, unloving, and rude. Is he correct?

As with most of Christ's critics, Mr. McKinsey is guilty of judging Jesus' words by what is common in twenty-first-century English vernacular, rather than putting Jesus' comments in their proper first-century setting. It was not rude or inappropriate for a man in the first century to speak to a lady by saying, "Woman (*gunai*)...." This "was a highly respectful and affectionate mode of address" (Vincent, 1997), "with no idea of censure" (Robertson, 1932, 5:34). The New

International Version correctly captures the meaning of this word in John 2:4: "**Dear woman**, why do you involve me?" (emp. added). Jesus used this word when complimenting the Syrophoenician woman's great faith (Matthew 15:28), when affectionately addressing Mary Magdalene after His resurrection (John 20: 15), and when speaking to His disconsolate mother one last time from the cross (John 19:26). Paul used this same word when addressing Christian women (1 Corinthians 7:16). As Adam Clarke noted: "[C]ertainly no kind of disrespect is intended, but, on the contrary, complaisance, affability, tenderness, and concern, and in this sense it is used in the best Greek writers" (1996).

As to why Jesus used the term "woman" (*gunai*) instead of "mother" (*meetros*) when speaking to Mary (which even in first-century Hebrew and Greek cultures was an unusual way to address one's mother), Leon Morris noted that Jesus most likely was indicating

> that there is a new relationship between them as he enters his public ministry.... Evidently Mary thought of the intimate relations of the home at Nazareth as persisting. But Jesus in his public ministry was not only or primarily the son of Mary, but "the Son of Man" who was to bring the realities of heaven to people on earth (1:51). A new relationship was established (1995, p. 159).

R.C.H. Lenski added: "[W]hile Mary will forever remain his [Jesus'—KB/EL] mother, in his calling Jesus knows no mother or earthly relative, he is their Lord and Savior as well as of all men. The common earthly relation is swallowed up in the divine" (1961b, p. 189). It is logical to conclude that Jesus was simply "informing" His mother in a loving manner that as He began performing miracles for the purpose of proving His deity and the divine origin of His message, His relationship to His mother was about to change.

Finally, the point also must be stressed that honoring fathers and mothers does not mean that a son or daughter never can correct his or her parents. Correction and honor are no more opposites than correction and love. One of the greatest ways parents disclose their love to their children is by correcting them when they make mistakes (Hebrews 12:6-9; Revelation 3:19). Similarly, one of the ways in which a mature son might honor his parents is by taking them aside when they have erred, and lovingly pointing out their mistake or oversight in a certain matter. Think how much more honorable this action would be than to take no action and allow them to continue in a path of error without informing them of such. We must keep in mind that even though Mary was a great woman "who found favor with God" (Luke 1:30), she was not perfect (cf. Romans 3:10,23). She was not God, nor the "mother of God" (viz., she did not originate Jesus or bring Him into existence). But, she was the one chosen to carry the Son of God in her womb. Who better to correct any misunderstanding she may have had than this Son?

Was Jesus Ignorant of the Old Testament?

When Jesus spoke to Nicodemus regarding the need to be "born again" (John 3:1-8), He also sought to impress upon the mind of this ruler of the Jews that His words were from above. Jesus spoke of spiritual things that no man knew (Matthew 13:35; cf. 7:28-29; Luke 2:47). One of the reasons Jesus gave for being able to expound on such spiritual truths is found in John 3: 13. Here, the apostle John recorded that Jesus said to Nicodemus, "No one has ascended to heaven but He who came down from heaven, that is, the Son of Man" (John 3:13). According to the skeptic, this statement by Jesus is severely flawed. Since the Old Testament reveals that Elijah escaped physical death and "went up by a whirlwind **into heaven**" (2 Kings 2:11; cf. Genesis 5:24; Hebrews 11:5), allegedly Jesus could not truthfully tell Nicodemus, "No one has ascended to heaven." Is the skeptic right?

For Jesus' statement to contradict what the Old Testament says about Elijah, one first must presuppose that Jesus was referring to the exact same place to which Elijah ascended. Can the skeptic be certain that the "heaven" to which Jesus referred, is the same one into which the body of Elijah ascended? The words "heaven" or "heavens" appear in our English Bibles about 700 times. And yet, in many of the passages where "heaven(s)" is found, the inspired writers were not discussing the spiritual heaven with which we most often associate the word. For example, in Genesis 1 and 2 the Hebrew word for heaven appears 15 times in 14 verses. Yet in every instance, the word is referring to something besides the spiritual heaven where God dwells. The word "heaven(s)" (Hebrew *shamayim*, Greek *ouranos*) is used by Bible writers in three different ways. It is used to refer to the atmospheric heavens in which the airplanes fly, the birds soar, and the clouds gather (Genesis 1:20; Jeremiah 4:25; Matthew 6:26, ASV). "Heaven(s)" also is used in the Bible when referring to the firmament where we find the Sun, Moon, and stars—the sidereal heavens, or outer space (Genesis

1:14-15; Psalm 19:4,6; Isaiah 13:10). The third "heaven" frequently mentioned in Scripture is the spiritual heaven in which Jehovah dwells (Psalm 2:4; Hebrews 9: 24), and where, one day, the faithful will live forevermore (Revelation 21:18-23; John 14:1-3). The context of John 3 clearly indicates that Jesus is referring to the spiritual heavens wherein God dwells (cf. John 3:27). The passage in 2 Kings 2:11, however, is not as clear. The writer of 2 Kings easily could have meant that the body of Elijah miraculously ascended up high into the air, never to be seen by anyone on Earth again. Nowhere does the text indicate that he left Earth at that moment to dwell in God's presence. He definitely went somewhere, but we have no evidence that he was transferred to the actual throne room of God Almighty.

The Bible indicates that when God's faithful servants leave this Earth, their spirits are taken to dwell in a place referred to as paradise (or "the bosom of Abraham"—Luke 16:19-31). Recall when Jesus was fastened to the cross, and told the penitent thief, "Today, you will be with Me in Paradise" (Luke 23:43). The word paradise is of Persian derivation, and means a "garden" or "park." Where was it that Jesus and the thief went? Neither of them went to heaven to be with God the Father on that very day, for in John 20:17 after His resurrection, Jesus reassured Mary that **He had not yet ascended to the Father**. So where did Jesus and the thief go after dying on the cross? Peter gave the answer to that question in his sermon in Acts 2 when he quoted Psalm 16. Acts 2:27 states that God would not abandon Christ's soul in **hades**, nor allow Christ to undergo decay. So while Christ's body was placed in a tomb for three days, Christ's spirit went to hades. [NOTE: The word hades occurs ten times in the New Testament, and always refers to the unseen realm of the dead—the receptacle of disembodied spirits where all people who die await the Lord's return and judgment. One part of hades, where Jesus and the thief went, is known as paradise.] Peter argued that David, who penned Psalm 16, was not referring to himself, since David's body was still in the tomb (Acts 2:29), and his spirit was still in the hadean realm (Acts 2:34). Acts 2 indicates that a faithful servant of God does not go directly to be with God the Father when he dies; rather, he goes to a holding place in hades known as paradise—the same place where Abraham went after he died (Luke 16:22ff.), and the same place where the spirit of Elijah went after he was caught up from the Earth. In short, the Bible does not teach that Elijah left Earth to begin immediately dwelling in the presence of the Father (where Jesus was before His incarnation—John 1:1). Thus, technically he did not ascend to the "place" whence Jesus came.

For the sake of argument, consider for a moment that the skeptic is right, and that Elijah's spirit did not go to paradise, but was taken to dwell in the very presence of God. Could Jesus still have made the statement He did, and yet not be inaccurate? We believe so. Notice again the response to Nicodemus' question, "How can these things be?" Jesus said: "If I have told you earthly things and you do not believe, how will you believe if I tell you heavenly things? **No one has ascended to heaven** but He who came down from heaven, that is, the Son of Man" (John 3:12-13, emp. added). It may be that Jesus meant nothing more than that no one has ever gone up to heaven "by his own act" or "on his own terms" (see Bullinger, 1898, pp. 281-282). Elijah and Enoch had been **taken** by God, which is different than freely ascending up into heaven by one's own ability. Furthermore, Jesus' words, "No one has ascended to heaven," also could have meant that no one has ever gone up into heaven to then return and speak firsthand about what he saw, and to spread the same saving message that Jesus preached. Jesus was emphasizing to Nicodemus how no one on Earth at that time was revealing such spiritual truths as Christ was, because no one ever had ascended to heaven only to return and talk about what he had seen and learned. Such seems to have been the main point Jesus was making in John 3:13. No one on Earth had seen what Jesus had seen, and thus could not teach what He taught.

Truly, the skeptic's accusation that Jesus either lied or was mistaken regarding his comment to Nicodemus about no one having ascended to heaven is unsubstantiated. Perhaps the word heaven used in 2 Kings 2:11 was not meant to convey the idea of the spiritual heavens in which God dwells. Or, considering the Bible's teaching on departed spirits of the righteous being in a holding place known as paradise, and not in the actual presence of Almighty God, Jesus could have meant that no person has ever ascended to the throne room of God from which He came. Furthermore, it also is interesting to note that Nicodemus, being "a man of the Pharisees" (John 3:1), and thus one who would have been very well acquainted with the details of the Old Testament, did not respond to Jesus by saying, "Wait a minute, Rabbi. What about Elijah and Enoch? Isn't it written in the law and prophets that they ascended to heaven?" Surely, had Jesus contradicted something in the law and the prophets, it would have been brought to His attention, especially by a Pharisee. Yet, the apostle John never recorded such a statement.

Admittedly, at first glance, it might appear as if the statements, "Elijah went up by a whirlwind into heaven" (2 Kings 2:11) and "No man has ascended to heaven" (John 3:13), are incongruous. However, when a person considers all of the possible solutions to the allegation that Jesus was ignorant of Elijah and Enoch's ascensions, he must admit that such a conclusion is unjustified.

Did Jesus Deny Moral Perfection?

Near the end of Jesus' earthly ministry, a wealthy young ruler (whose name remains anonymous) came running to Jesus with an urgent question. When he finally reached Him, the young man humbly knelt before the Christ and asked, "Good Teacher, what shall I do that I may inherit eternal life?" (Mark 10: 17). Before Jesus answered the gentleman's question, He first responded by saying, "Why do you call Me good? No one is good but One, that is, God" (Mark 10:18). Jesus then proceeded to answer the rich man's question by instructing him to keep the commandments of God.

What did Jesus mean when He stated that "no one is good but One, that is, God"? Was the Lord's question intended to teach that no one else but God ought to be called "good"? Was His question ("Why do you call me good?") asked because He did not believe He was good in the sense of God being good? Skeptics charge that Jesus was denying moral perfection—that

He was not really God in the flesh like so many had claimed (cf. Matthew 16:16; John 20:28; etc.). What is the truth of the matter?

First of all, Jesus was not teaching that we can never describe others by using the adjective "good." If so, then this contradicts not only other statements by Jesus, but also the rest of Scripture. The psalmist stated that the man who "deals graciously and lends" is "a good man" (Psalm 112:5). The wise man said that one who "leaves an inheritance to his children's children" is "a good man" (Proverbs 13:22). In his history of the early church, Luke recorded that "Barnabas was a good man" (Acts 11:24). Even Jesus stated previous to His encounter with the rich young ruler that "a good man out of the good treasure of his heart, brings forth good things" (Matthew 12:35). Thus, when Jesus spoke to the wealthy ruler He was not using "good" in the sense of a **man** being "good." Rather, He was using it in the sense of **God** being "**supremely good**." The kind of goodness to which He was referring belonged only to God.

We understand that Jesus did **not** mean that we must expunge the word "good" from all conversations unless we are describing God. But was Christ implying that He was not God or that He was not morally perfect? No. Jesus indicated on several other occasions that He was deity (cf. Mark 14:62; John 9:36-38; 10:10; etc.), and so His statements recorded in Mark 10:17-22 (as well as Matthew 19:16-22 and Luke 18:18-23) certainly were not meant to discredit His Godhood. Furthermore, the Bible reveals that Jesus never sinned—i.e., He was morally perfect. He "was in all points tempted as we are, yet without sin" (Hebrews 4:15).

Jesus "committed no sin, nor was deceit found in His mouth" (1 Peter 2:22). In His conversation with the rich ruler, Jesus did not intend to deny divinity, but instead was actually asserting that He was God (and thus morally perfect). Jesus simply wanted this young man to appreciate the significance of the title he had employed, and to realize to Whom he was speaking. In short, Christ's words could be paraphrased thusly: "Do you know the meaning of this word you apply to me and which you use so freely? There is none good save God; if you apply that term to me, and you understand what you mean, you affirm that I am God" (Foster, 1971, p. 1022.).

Was Jesus a Hypocrite?

A man who instructs a person to refrain from doing something he deems inappropriate, but then proceeds to do the very thing he forbade the other person to do, is considered a hypocrite. A preacher who teaches about the sinfulness of drunkenness (cf. Galatians 5:21), but then is seen a short while later stumbling down the street, intoxicated with alcohol, could be accused of being guilty of hypocrisy. Some have accused Jesus of such insincere teaching. Allegedly, in the very sermon in which He condemned the Pharisees for their unrighteousness (Matthew 5:20), Jesus revealed His own sinfulness by way of condemning those who used a word He sometimes uttered. Based upon His forbiddance of the use of the word "fool" in Matthew 5:22, and His use of this word elsewhere, skeptics have asserted that Jesus (Who the Bible claims "committed no sin, nor was deceit found in His mouth"—1 Peter 2:22; cf. 2 Corinthians 5:21), was guilty of hypocrisy (see Morgan, 2003; Wells, 2001). In Matthew 5:21-22, Jesus stated:

> You have heard that it was said to those of old, "You shall not murder, and whoever murders will be in danger of the judgment." But I say to you that whoever is angry with his brother without a cause shall be in danger of the judgment. And whoever says to his brother, "Raca!" shall be in danger of the council. But **whoever says, "You fool!" shall be in danger of hell fire** (Matthew 5:21-22, emp. added).

Whereas in this passage Jesus warned against the use of the word "fool," in other passages Jesus openly used this term to describe various people. Near the end of the Sermon on the Mount, Jesus likened the person who heard His teachings, but did not follow them, to "**a foolish man** who built his house on the sand" (Matthew 7:26). When teaching about the need to be prepared for His second coming, Jesus compared those who were not ready for His return to **five foolish virgins** (Matthew 25:1-12). Then, while Jesus was condemning the Pharisees for their inconsistency in matters of religion, He stated: "Woe to you, blind guides, who say, 'Whoever swears by the temple, it is nothing; but whoever swears by the gold of the temple, he is obliged to perform it.' **Fools and blind!** For which is greater, the gold or the temple that sanctifies the gold?" (Matthew 23:16-17; cf. 23:18-19). The question that some ask in response to these alleged hypocritical statements is, "How could Jesus condemn the use of the word 'fool' in Matthew 5:22, but then proceed to use this word Himself on other occasions?"

First, for Jesus' statement in Matthew 5:22 to contradict His actions recorded in other passages, the skeptic must prove that the term "fool," as used in 5:22, is the same word used elsewhere. The Greek word "Raca," used earlier in Matthew 5:22, is a transliteration of the Aramaic term whose precise meaning is disputed. [Most likely, it means "an empty one who acts as a numskull" (Lenski, 1961a, p. 219; cf. also Robertson, 1930, 1:44).] The exact meaning of the term "fool" (Greek *more*) in this context also is debated. "Most scholars take it, as the ancient Syrian versions did, to mean **you fool**" (Bauer, et al., 1957, p. 533, emp. in orig.). Although some assume that *more* is the vocative of the Greek *moros*, in all likelihood,

> just as "Raca" is a non-Greek word, so is the word *more* that Jesus used here. If so, then it is a word which to a Jewish ear meant "rebel (against God)" or "apostate"; it was the word which Moses in exasperation used to the disaffected Israelites in the wilderness of Zin... (Numbers 20:10). For these rash words, uttered under intense provocation, Moses was excluded from the Promised Land (Kaiser, et al., 1996, p. 359).

Thus, it is quite possible that *more* (translated "[Y]ou fool" in Matthew 5:22) is not the normal Greek *moros* (fool) that Jesus applied to the Pharisees on other occasions (Matthew 23:17,19), but represents the Hebrew *moreh* (cf. Numbers 20:10). [For this reason, translators of the American Standard Version added a marginal note to this word in Matthew 5:22: "Or, ***Moreh*****, a Hebrew expression of condemnation**."] Obviously, if two different words are under consideration, Jesus logically could not be considered a hypocrite.

Second, it must be remembered that Jesus' comments in Matthew 5:22 were made within a context where He was condemning unrighteous anger (5:21-26). Whereas the Pharisees condemned murder, but overlooked the evil emotions and attitudes that sometimes led to the shedding of innocent blood, Jesus condemned both the actions and the thoughts. Instead of dealing with only "peripheral" problems, Jesus went to the heart of the matter. As someone Who "knew what was in man" (John 2:25), Jesus was more than qualified to pronounce judgment upon the hypocritical Pharisees (cf. John 12:48). Like the unrighteousness that characterized the Pharisees' charitable deeds (Matthew 6:1-4), prayers (6:5-15), fasting (6:16-18), and judgments (7:1-5), Jesus also condemned their unrighteous anger. [NOTE: Jesus did not condemn **all** anger (cf. Ephesians 4:26; John 2:13-17), only **unrighteous** anger.] It was in this context that Jesus warned against the use of the word "fool." Jesus was not prohibiting a person from calling people "fools" if it was done in an appropriate manner (cf. Psalm 14:1), but He was forbidding it when done in the spirit of malicious contempt. He "warned against using the word fool as a form of abuse" that indicated "hatred in one's heart toward others" ("Fool," 1986; cf. Matthew 5:43-48). As in many other situations, it seems that the attitude, rather than actual words, is the focus of the prohibition.

While this verse, when taken in its context, is seen to be consistent with Jesus' words and actions recorded elsewhere in the gospel accounts, His prohibition regarding the **manner** of a word's usage should not be overlooked in the apologist's effort to defend the deity of Christ (or any other Bible doctrine). We may call an atheist a "fool" for not acknowledging God's existence (Psalm 14:1), but to do so in a hateful, malicious manner is sinful. Remember, the Christian is called to "give a defense to everyone" in a spirit of "meekness and fear" (1 Peter 3:15).

Did Jesus Encourage Thievery?

Numerous passages of Scripture teach—either explicitly or implicitly—about the sinfulness of thievery. One of the Ten Commandments that God gave to Israel was: "You shall not steal" (Exodus 20:15). In the book of Leviticus, one can read where "the Lord spoke to Moses, saying, 'Speak to all the congregation of the children of Israel, and say to them... You shall not steal, nor deal falsely, nor lie to one another.... You shall not cheat your neighbor, nor rob him' " (19: 1-2,11,13). If a thief was found breaking into a house at night and was struck so that he died, the old law stated that there would be "no guilt for his bloodshed" (Exodus 22:2). Under the new covenant, the apostle Paul wrote to the church at Ephesus, saying, "Let him who stole steal no longer, but rather let him labor, working with his hands what is good, that he may have something to give him who has need" (4:28). And to the Christians at Corinth, Paul wrote that thieves "will not inherit the kingdom of God" (1 Corinthians 6:9-11). Thus, God obviously considers stealing to be a transgression of His law.

Critics of the deity of Christ, however, assert that Jesus once commanded His disciples to steal a donkey and a colt prior to entering Jerusalem during the final week of His life. According to Matthew's gospel account, Jesus instructed His disciples, saying, "Go into the village opposite you, and immediately you will find a donkey tied, and a colt with her. Loose them and bring them to Me. And if anyone says anything to you, you shall say, 'The Lord has need of them,' and immediately he will send them" (Matthew 21:1-3). Luke added: "So those who were sent went their way and found it just as He had said to them. But as they were loosing the colt, the owners of it said to them, 'Why are you loosing the colt?' And they said, 'The Lord has need of him.' Then they brought him to Jesus" (Luke 19:32-35). Regarding this story, skeptic Dennis McKinsey asked: "Are we to believe this isn't theft? Imagine seeing a stranger driving your car away while claiming the lord needed it" (1985, p. 1). Allegedly, "Jesus told people to take a colt...without the owners' permission." And that, says McKinsey, is "commonly known as stealing" (2000, p. 236). Another infidel by the name of Dan Barker commented on this event in the life of Jesus in his book, *Losing Faith in Faith: From Preacher to Atheist*, saying, "I was taught as a child that when you take something without asking for it, that is stealing" (1992, p. 166). But did Jesus really encourage His disciples to **steal** a donkey and a colt? Can His actions be explained logically in light of the numerous statements throughout Scripture that clearly condemn thievery?

Before responding to these criticisms, consider the following: If a husband were to e-mail his wife and ask her to walk to a neighbor's house and pick up his truck so that he could use it to haul an old furnace to the junkyard, would someone who read his e-mail (perhaps finding a hard copy of it crumpled up in the trash) be justified in concluding that this gentleman asked his wife to steal the truck? Certainly not. Since the e-mail had no other information in it than a request for the wife concerning a neighbor's truck, a person reading the note would have to have access to additional information in order to come to the conclusion that this man and his wife were guilty of theft. The reader may be ignorant of the fact that the husband had prearranged such a pick-up with his neighbor the previous day. Or, perhaps the neighbor had told the husband at some earlier time that he could use his truck whenever he needed it.

What Mr. McKinsey and other skeptics never seem to take into consideration in their interpretation of Scripture is that the Bible does not record every single detail of every event it mentions (cf. John 21:25). The Bible was not intended to be an exhaustive chronological timeline citing every detail about the lives of all of the men and women mentioned within it. The New Testament book of Acts covers a period of about thirty years, but it actually is only about **some** of the acts of **some** of the early Christians. There were many more things that Paul, Peter, Silas, Luke, and other first-century Christians did that are not recorded therein. For example, Paul spent three years in Arabia and Damascus after his conversion (Galatians 1:16-18), yet Luke did not mention this detail, nor the many things Paul accomplished during these three years.

The case of Jesus telling His disciples to go locate the donkey and colt does not prove thievery, any more than Jesus' disciples inquiring about and occupying an "upper room" makes them trespassers (cf. Mark 14:13-15). When sending His two disciples to get the requested animals, Jesus told them exactly where to go and what to say, as if He already knew the circumstances under which the donkey and colt were available. Jesus may very well have prearranged for the use of the donkeys. Neither Mr. McKinsey nor any other skeptic can prove otherwise. Similar to how a man is not obligated to go home from work every night and rehearse to his wife **everything** he did **each hour** at work, the Bible is not obligated to fill in every detail of every event, including the one regarding the attainment of two donkeys. No contradiction or charge of wrong is legitimate if unrelated circumstantial details may be postulated that account for explicit information that is given.

Furthermore, the innocence of Jesus and His disciples is reinforced by the fact that the disciples were able to leave with the donkeys. Had the disciples really been stealing the animals, one would think that the owners would not have allowed such to happen. Also, nothing is said in the text about what happened to the animals after Jesus rode them into Jerusalem. For all we know, Jesus' disciples could have immediately taken the animals back to their owners.

Skeptics who accuse the Lord of thievery have no solid ground upon which to stand. Unless it can be proven that Jesus' disciples took the donkeys by force (and without prior permission), justice demands that the accusations of guilt must be withdrawn.

In What Way was God Greater Than Jesus?

Since many passages in the New Testament indicate that Jesus was divine, and not just a man or an angel (cf. John 1:1,14; 10:30; Hebrews 1:5-14), some see an inconsistency with statements such as that found in John 14:28, in which Jesus declared: "My Father is greater than I" (John 14:28). Allegedly, this verse (among others—cf. 1 Corinthians 11:3; Mark 13:32; Colossians 3:1) proves that Jesus and the Bible writers were contradictory in their portrayal of Jesus' divine nature. Jesus could not be **one with God** and **lesser than God** at the same time, could He? What is the proper way to understand John 14:28?

Statements found in passages like John 14:28 (indicating that Jesus was lesser than God), or in Mark 13:32 (where Jesus made the comment that even He did not know on what day the Second Coming would be), must be understood in light of what the apostle Paul wrote to the church at Philippi concerning Jesus' self-limitation during His time on Earth. Christ,

> being in the form of God, did not consider it robbery to be equal with God, but **made Himself of no reputation** [**He "emptied Himself"**—NASB], taking the form of a bondservant, and coming in the likeness of men. And being found in appearance as a man, **He humbled Himself** and became obedient to the point of death, even the death of the cross (Philippians 2:6-8, emp. added).

While on Earth, and in the flesh, Jesus was **voluntarily** in a subordinate position to the Father. Christ "emptied Himself" (Philippians 2:7; He "made **Himself** nothing"—NIV). Unlike Adam and Eve, who made an attempt to seize equality with God (Genesis 3:5), Jesus, the last Adam (1 Corinthians 15:47), humbled Himself, and obediently accepted the role of a servant. Jesus' earthly limitations (cf. Mark 13:32), however, were not the consequence of a less-than-God **nature**; rather, they were the result of a **self-imposed**

submission reflecting the exercise of His sovereign will. While on Earth, Jesus assumed a position of complete subjection to the Father, and exercised His divine attributes only at the Father's bidding (cf. John 8:26,28-29) [*Wycliffe*..., 1985]. As A.H. Strong similarly commented many years ago, Jesus "resigned not the possession, nor yet entirely the use, but rather the independent exercise, of the divine attributes" (1907, p. 703).

Admittedly, understanding Jesus as being 100% God and 100% human is not an easy concept to grasp. When Jesus came to Earth, He added humanity to His divinity (He was "made in the likeness of men"). For the first time ever, He was subject to such things as hunger, thirst, growth (both physical and mental), pain, disease, and temptation (cf. Hebrews 4:15; Luke 2:52). At the same time Jesus added humanity to His divinity, however, He put Himself in a subordinate position to the Father in terms of role function (1 Corinthians 11:3). In short, when Jesus affirmed, "The Father is greater than I" (John 14:28), He was not denying His divine nature; rather, He was asserting that He had subjected Himself voluntarily to the Father's will.

AFTERWORD

After boasting that he would die with Jesus, the apostle Peter succumbed to the tempter's snare to deny the Lord. Peter not only denied the Lord once, but **three** times, and, when given the opportunity to identify himself with the Christ, crumbled under the weight of temptation. Luke, in his account of the Gospel, gives us a glimpse into one of the most powerful scenes in the Bible, as he describes what happened to Peter that night. As Peter finished denying the Lord for the third time, the rooster crowed, "and the Lord turned and looked at Peter. And Peter remembered the word of the Lord..." (Luke 22:61). Imagine those penetrating, loving eyes looking into Peter's helpless, sinful, self-loathing soul. What else was there for Peter to do but go out and weep bitterly? The love and pain in the eyes of the Savior acted as a penetrating beam of spiritual energy that melted the honest-yet-sinful heart of Peter.

This book has touched briefly on the power of the Savior. He lived in history, and He impacted humanity more than any figure ever to have existed. His sinless, matchless, physical life was snuffed out by those who had delivered Him up because of envy. The tomb in which His mangled body rested for three days was found empty on that glorious Sunday almost 2,000 years ago—exactly as the prophets had predicted. His resurrection, the crowning miracle of His earthly existence, proved that He was God in the flesh. His historically documented story was the ultimate answer to the problem of sin that countless generations throughout history had been seeking. And there He is, the Savior, staring into our mind's eye with all the love and pain that brought the apostle Peter to his knees. The only question left for us to ask is simply, "What will we do with Jesus?"

Will you reject the Son of God as your Lord and Savior as so many of the hardened Pharisees did in the first century? Will you verbally claim to follow Him, but really never dedicate your life to Him as millions of professed believers are doing today (cf. Matthew 7:21-23; 16:24-26)? Or, will you submit to Him and become a genuine Christian?

Unfortunately, some have come to the conclusion that man plays no part in his being saved from sin by God. They believe that there simply is nothing for them to do. Some simply think that the life of Jesus does not demand a response from us. The truth is, however, when it comes to the free gift of salvation that God extends to the whole world through His Son (John 3:16), there are requirements that must be met on the part of man in order for him to receive the gift of salvation. Similar to a man who might freely be given $1,000,000, but who still must "do" certain things in order to receive the money (e.g., pick up the check at a particular location, take the check to the bank, sign it, cash it, etc.), a non-Christian sinner must **do** some things to be saved.

The Ethiopian eunuch responded to Philip's preaching of Jesus by **doing** something (Acts 8:35-38). The Jews on Pentecost understood this point, as is evident by their question: "Men and brethren, what shall we **do**?" (Acts 2:37). Saul, later called Paul (Acts 13:9), believed that there was something else he needed to do besides experience a personal encounter with the resurrected Lord on his way to Damascus, for he asked Jesus, "Lord, what do You want me to **do**?" (Acts 9:6). And the jailor at Philippi, after observing the righteousness of Paul and Silas and being awakened by the earthquake to see the prison doors opened (Acts 16:20-29), "fell down trembling before Paul and Silas... and said, 'Sirs, what must I **do** to be saved?' " (Acts 16:30). If those who responded to these questions (Peter in Acts 2, Jesus in Acts 9, and Paul and Silas in Acts 16) had the mindset of some today, they should have answered by saying, "There is nothing for you to do. Just wait, and salvation will come to you." But their responses were quite different from this. All three times the question was asked, a command to **do** something was given. Peter told those on Pentecost to "repent and be baptized" (Acts 2:38); Paul and Silas instructed the Philippian jailor and his household to "[b]elieve on the Lord Jesus Christ" (Acts 16:31); and Jesus commanded Saul to "[a]rise and go into the city, and you will be told what you must do" (Acts 9:6). Notice that none of them gave the impression that salvation involves us "doing **nothing**." Jesus told Saul that he **"must do"** something. When Saul arrived in Damascus as Jesus had directed him, he did exactly what God's spokesman, Ananias, commanded him to do (Acts 22:12-16; 9:17-18).

The New Testament gives specific prerequisites that must be followed before one can receive the atoning benefit of Christ's blood (Revelation 1:5; 1 John 1:7). These conditions are neither vague nor difficult to understand. A person must **confess faith** in Jesus Christ as the Son of God (John 8:24; Romans 10:9-

10; cf. 1 Timothy 6:12), and he must **turn away** from his past sins (Acts 26:20; Luke 13:3; Acts 2:38). However, that is not the end of the matter. The Bible discusses yet another step that precedes the reception of the gift of salvation—a step that has become unquestionably controversial within Christendom—**water baptism**. It is mentioned numerous times throughout the New Testament, and both Jesus and His disciples taught that it **precedes** salvation (Mark 16:16; Matthew 28:19-20; Acts 2:38). The apostle Paul's sins were washed away only **after** he was immersed in water (Acts 22:16; cf. Acts 9:18). [NOTE: Even though it was on the road to Damascus that Paul heard the Lord, spoke to Him, and believed on Him (Acts 9), Paul did not receive salvation until he went into Damascus and was baptized.] The book of Acts is replete with examples of those who did not receive the gift of salvation until after they professed faith in Christ, repented of their sins, and were baptized (Acts 2:38-41; 8:12; 8: 26-40; 10:34-48; 16:14-15; 16:30-34; 18:8). Furthermore, the epistles of Peter and Paul also call attention to the necessity of baptism (1 Peter 3:21; Colossians 2:12; Romans 6:1-4). If a person wants the multitude of spiritual blessings found "in Christ" (e.g., salvation—2 Timothy 2:10; forgiveness—Ephesians 1:7; cf. Ephesians 2:12; etc.), he must not stop after confessing faith in the Lord Jesus, or after resolving within himself to turn from a sinful lifestyle. He also must be "baptized **into** Christ" (Galatians 3:27; Romans 6:3) "for the remission of sins" (Acts 2:38). It is at this point that God washes away (Acts 22:16) the sins of an alien sinner by the blood of Jesus Christ (1 Peter 1:18-19; Revelation 1:5).

If you are not a Christian, it is our prayer that you will become one today by responding in faith to what Jesus did for you, just as non-Christians did some 2,000 years ago. If you are a Christian, we encourage you to remain faithful to the Lord, "knowing that your labor is not in vain in the Lord" (1 Corinthians 15:58; Revelation 2:10).

Throughout human history, billions of people have been born, lived, and died. Should the world remain much longer, billions more will come and go. But there is only one person, one name, that has the power to save the world from sin and death. Only one personality in all of human history was able to live a perfect life and establish a kingdom that will never be destroyed. Only one man had the power to conquer death and set humans free from its captivating grasp. The words of Peter ring as true today as they did almost 20 centuries ago: "[T]here is no other name under heaven given among men by which we must be saved" (Acts 4:12). Jesus Christ stands alone as the only One that can offer eternal salvation.

REFERENCES

The American Heritage Dictionary of the English Language (2000), (Boston, MA: Houghton Mifflin), fourth edition.

Anderson, J.N.D. (1969), *Christianity: The Witness of History* (London: Tyndale).

Anderson, Norman (1985), *Jesus Christ: The Witness of History* (Downers Grove, IL: InterVarsity Press), second edition.

Andy (1998), "No Greater Sacrifice," *Widdershins*, 4[4], [On-line], URL: http://www.widdershins.org/vol4iss4/01.htm.

Ankerberg, John, John Weldon, and Walter Kaiser (1989), *The Case for Jesus the Messiah* (Chattanooga, TN: John Ankerberg Evangelistic Association).

Augustine of Hippo (no date), *Christian Doctrine*, [On-line], URL: http://www.newadvent.org/fathers/12022.htm.

Bales, James D. (no date), *The Originality of Christ* (Searcy, AR: Privately published by author).

Barker, Dan (1992), *Losing Faith in Faith* (Minneapolis, MN: Freedom From Religion Foundation).

Baron, David (2000 reprint), *Rays of Messiah's Glory* (Jerusalem, Israel: Kern Ahvah Meshihit).

Bauer, Walter, William Arndt, and F.W. Gingrich (1957), *A Greek-English Lexicon of the New Testament and Other Early Christian Literature* (Chicago, IL: University of Chicago Press).

Beare, Francis Wright (1962), *The Earliest Records of Jesus* (New York, NY: Abingdon).

Blaiklock, E.M. (1984), *The Archaeology of the New Testament* (Grand Rapids, MI: Zondervan), revised edition.

Blomberg, Craig L. (1987), *The Historical Reliability of the Gospels* (Downers Grove, IL: InterVarsity Press).

Bonz, Marianne (1998), "Recovering the Material World of the Early Christians," [On-line], URL: http://www.pbs.org/wgbh/pages/frontline/shows/religion/maps/arch/recovering.html.

Briggs, Charles A. (1988 reprint), *Messianic Prophecy: The Prediction of the Fulfillment of Redemption through the Messiah* (Peabody, MA: Hendrickson).

Bruce, F.F. (1953), *The New Testament Documents–Are They Reliable?* (Grand Rapids, MI: Eerdmans), fourth edition.

Bruce, F.F. (1967), *The New Testament Documents–Are They Reliable?* (Grand Rapids, MI: Eerdmans), fifth edition.

Bruce, F.F. (1990), *The Book of Acts* (Grand Rapids, MI: Eerdmans), third revised edition.

Budge, E.A. Wallis, Trans. (1960), *Papyrus of Ani: The Egyptian Book of the Dead* (New York, NY: Gramercy, 1999 reprint).

Bullinger, E.W. (1898), *Figures of Speech Used in the Bible* (Grand Rapids, MI: Baker, 1968 reprint).

Carrier, Richard (2000), [On-line], URL: http://www.infidels.Org/library/modern/richard_carrier/resurrection/1b.html.

Case, Shirley Jackson (1909), "The Resurrection Faith of the First Disciples," *American Journal of Theology*, pp. 171-172, April.

Chapman, Colin (1981), *The Case for Christianity* (Grand Rapids, MI: Eerdmans).

Clarke, Adam (1996), *Adam Clarke's Commentary* (Electronic Database: Biblesoft).

Clement of Rome (no date), *First Epistle to the Corinthians*, [On-line], URL: http://www.newadvent.org/fathers/1010.htm.

Clements, Tad S. (1990), *Science vs. Religion* (Buffalo, NY: Prometheus).

Coffman, James Burton (1984), *Commentary on the Gospel of Matthew* (Abilene, TX: ACU Press).

Cohen, Robert M. (no date), "Why I Know Yeshua is the Jewish Messiah," [On-line], URL: http://www.imja.com/Atonem.html.

Cornfield, Gaalyah, ed. (1982), *The Historical Jesus* (New York, NY: Macmillan).

Curr, Henry S. (1941), "The Intrinsic Credibility of Biblical Miracles," *Bibliotheca Sacra*, 98:470-479, October.

Darrow, Clarence and Wallace Rice (1929), *Infidels and Heretics: An Agnostic's Anthology* (Boston, MA: Stratford).

Davis, Wendy (1995), "As Old as the Moon: Sacrifice in History," *Widdershins*, 1[2], June 21, [On-line], URL: http://www.widdershins.org/vol1iss2/10.htm.

DeHoff, George W. (1944), *Why We Believe the Bible* (Murfreesboro, TN: DeHoff).

"Dionysus and Yeshua" (no date), [On-line], URL: http://www.dhushara.com/book/diochris/dio2.htm.

Doane, T.W. (1882), *Bible Myths and Their Parallels in Other Religions* (Kila, MT: Kessinger).

Dummelow, J.R. (1937), *One Volume Commentary* (New York: MacMillan).

Durant, Will, ed. (1932), *On the Meaning of Life* (New York: Long and Smith).

Eaves, Thomas F. (1980), "The Inspired Word," *Great Doctrines of the Bible*, ed. M.H. Tucker (Knoxville, TN: East Tennessee School of Preaching).

Eusebius (no date), *Ecclesiastical History*, [On-line], URL: http://www. newadvent.org/fathers/2501.htm.

Faber-Kaiser, A. (1977), *Jesus Died In Kashmir* (London: Gordon & Cremonsei).

Finegan, Jack (1959), *Light from the Ancient Past* (Princeton, NJ: Princeton University Press), second edition.

Finegan, Jack (1992), *The Archeology of the New Testament* (Princeton, NJ: Princeton University Press), revised edition.

Finegan, Jack (1998), *Handbook of Biblical Chronology* (Peabody, MA: Hendrickson).

"Fool," (1986), *Nelson's Illustrated Bible Dictionary* (Electronic Database: Biblesoft).

Forbush, William B., ed. (1954), *Fox's Book of Martyrs* (Grand Rapids, MI: Zondervan).

Foster, R.C. (1971), *Studies in the Life of Christ* (Grand Rapids, MI: Baker).

Free, Joseph P. and Howard F. Vos (1992), *Archaeology and Bible History* (Grand Rapids, MI: Zondervan).

Franklin, Stephen T. (1993), "Theological Foundations for the Uniqueness of Christ as Hope and Judge," *Evangelical Review of Theology*, 17[1]:29-53, January.

Freke, Timothy and Peter Gandy (1999), *The Jesus Mysteries* (New York: Harmony Books).

Gauvin, Marshall (1995-2005), "Did Jesus Christ Really Live?", [On-line], URL: http://www.infidels.org/library/historical/marshall_gauvin/did_jesus_really_live.html.

Geisler, Norman L. (1976), *Christian Apologetics* (Grand Rapids, MI: Baker).

Geisler, Norman L. and Ronald M. Brooks (1990), *When Skeptics Ask* (Wheaton, IL: Victor).

Graves, Kersey (1875), *The World's Sixteen Crucified Saviors* (Escondido, CA: The Book Tree, 1999 reprint).

Graves, Robert (1960), *The Greek Myths* (New York, NY: Penguin).

Guthrie, Donald (1990), *New Testament Introduction* (Downers Grove, IL: InterVarsity Press).

Habermas, Gary (1996), *The Historical Jesus* (Joplin, MO: College Press).

Habermas, Gary (2001), "Why I Believe the Miracles of Jesus Actually Happened," *Why I am a Christian*, eds. Norman L. Geisler and Paul K. Hoffman (Grand Rapids, MI: Baker).

Harvey, A.E. (1982), *Jesus and the Constraints of History* (Philadelphia, PA: Westminster).

Horne, Thomas H. (1841), *An Introduction to the Critical Study and Knowledge of the Holy Scriptures* (Grand Rapids, MI: Baker, 1970 reprint).

Huffman, J.A. (1956), *The Messianic Hope in Both Testaments* (Butler, IN: Higley Press).

Hughes, J.J. (1986), "Paulus, Sergius," *International Standard Bible Encyclopedia*, ed. Geoffrey W. Bromiley (Grand Rapids, MI: Eerdmans), revised edition.

Huxley, Julian (1960), "The Evolutionary Vision," *Issues in Evolution* [Volume 3 of *Evolution After Darwin*], ed. Sol Tax (Chicago, IL: University of Chicago Press).

Irenaeus (no date), "Fragments from the Lost Writings of Irenaeus," [On-line], URL: http://www.newadvent.org/fathers/0134.htm.

Jackson, Wayne (1982), "He Showed Himself Alive by Many Proofs," *Reason & Revelation*, 1:33-35, August.

Jackson, Wayne (1991a), "The Holy Bible–Inspired of God," *Christian Courier*, 27:1-3, May.

Jackson, Wayne (1991b), "Josephus and the Bible [Part II]" *Reason & Revelation*, 11:29-32, August.

Jamieson, Robert, et al. (1997), *Jamieson, Fausset, and Brown Bible Commentary* (Electronic Database: Biblesoft).

Josephus, Flavius (1987 reprint), *The Life and Works of Flavius Josephus*, trans. William Whitson (Peabody, MA: Hendrickson).

Justin Martyr (no date), *Dialogue with Trypho*, [On-line], URL: http://www.newadvent.org/fathers/01283.htm.

Justin Martyr (no date), *First Apology,* [On-line], URL: http://www.newadvent.org/fathers/0126.htm.

Kähler, Martin (1896), *The So-called Historical Jesus and the Historic, Biblical Christ*, trans. Carl E. Braaten (Philadelphia, PA: Fortress, 1964 reprint).

Kaiser, Walter (1995), *The Messiah in the Old Testament* (Grand Rapids, MI: Zondervan).

Kaiser, Walter C. Jr., Peter H. Davids, F.F. Bruce, and Manfred T. Brauch (1996), *Hard Sayings of the Bible* (Downers Grove, IL: InterVarsity Press).

Kearley, F. Furman (1976), "The Miracles of Jesus," *Firm Foundation*, 93[27]:4, July 6.

Kennedy, D. James and Jerry Newcombe (1994), *What If Christ Had Never Been Born?* (Nashville, TN: Nelson).

Key, Howard Clark (1970), *Jesus in History* (New York, NY: Harcourt, Brace and World).

Kligerman, Aaron (1957), *Old Testament Messianic Prophecy* (Grand Rapids, MI: Zondervan).

Knight, K. (2004), "The Fathers of the Church," [On-line], URL: http://www.newadvent.org/fathers/.

Lenski, R.C.H. (1961a), *The Interpretation of St. Matthew's Gospel* (Minneapolis, MN: Augsburg).

Lenski, R.C.H. (1961b), *The Interpretation of St. John's Gospel* (Minneapolis, MN: Augsburg).

Lewis, C.S. (1970), *God in the Dock*, ed. Walter Hooper (Grand Rapids, MI: Eerdmans).

Lewis, C.S. (1975), *Miracles* (New York, NY: Touchstone).

Linton, Irwin H. (1943), *A Lawyer Examines the Bible* (Grand Rapids, MI: Baker), sixth edition.

The Lost Books of the Bible (1979 reprint), (New York, NY: Random House).

Lowder, Jeffrey Jay (2000), "Josh McDowell's 'Evidence' for Jesus: Is It Reliable?", [On-line], URL: http://www.infidels.org/library/modern/jeff_lowder/jury/chap5.html.

Lyman, Eric J. (2006), "Italian Atheist Sues Priest Over Jesus' Existence," *USA Today*, January 31, 8A.

Maier, Paul L. (1991), *In the Fullness of Time: A Historian Looks at Christmas, Easter, and the Early Church* (San Francisco, CA: Harper Collins).

McCabe, Joseph (1926), *The Myth of the Resurrection and Other Essays* (Amherst, NY: Prometheus, 1993 reprint).

McClintock, John and James Strong (1968 reprint), "Cyprus," *Cyclopaedia of Biblical, Theological, and Ecclesiastical Literature* (Grand Rapids, MI: Baker).

McGarvey, J.W. (no date), *The Fourfold Gospel* (Cincinnati, OH: Standard).

McGarvey, J.W. (no date), *New Commentary on Acts of Apostles* (Delight, AR: Gospel Light).

McGarvey, J.W. (1875), *The New Testament Commentary: Matthew and Mark* (Delight, AR: Gospel Light).

McKinsey, C. Dennis (no date), "Jesus, Imperfect Beacon," *Biblical Errancy,* [On-line], URL: http://members.aol.com/ckbloomfld/bepart11.html#issref113.

McKinsey, C. Dennis (no date), "Problems with the Credentials and Character of Jesus," *Biblical Errancy,* [On-line], URL: http://mywebpages.comcast.net/errancy/issues/iss190.htm.

McKinsey, C. Dennis (1983), "Commentary," *Biblical Errancy,* pp. 1-4, February.

McKinsey, C. Dennis (1985), "Commentary," *Biblical Errancy,* pp. 1-2, January.

McKinsey, C. Dennis (1995), *The Encyclopedia of Biblical Errancy* (Amherst, NY: Prometheus).

McKinsey, C. Dennis (2000), *Biblical Errancy* (Amherst, NY: Prometheus).

McRay, John (1991), *Archaeology and the New* Testament (Grand Rapids, MI: Baker).

Meier, John P. (1990), "Jesus in Josephus: A Modest Proposal," *The Catholic Biblical Quarterly*, 52:76-99.

Metzger, Bruce M. (1968), *The Text of the New Testament* (New York, NY: Oxford University Press).

Metzger, Bruce (1993), "The Jewish Targums," *Bibliotheca Sacra*, 150:35ff., January, [On-line], URL: http://www.bible-researcher.com/aramaic4.html.

Monser, J.W. (1961), *An Encyclopedia on the Evidences; or Masterpieces of Many Minds* (Grand Rapids, MI: Baker).

Montgomery, John Warwick (1964), *History and Christianity* (Downers Grove, IL: InterVarsity).

Morgan, Donald (2003), "Was Jesus a Hypocrite?" [On-line], URL: http://www.infidels.org/library/modern/donald_morgan/hypocrite.shtml.

Morris, Leon (1995), *The Gospel According to John* (Grand Rapids, MI: Eerdmans), revised edition.

Origen (no date), *Against Celsus*, [On-line], URL: http://www.newadvent.org/fathers/04161.htm.

"Osiris" (1997), *Encyclopaedia Britannica* (London: Encyclopaedia Britannica, Inc.).

Owen, Richard (2006), "Prove Christ Exists, Judge Orders Priest," *The Times Online*, January 3, [On-line], URL: http://www.timesonline.co.uk/article/0,,13509-1967413,00.html.

Parsons, John (2003-2006), "Hebrew Names of God: The Mashiach as Revealed in the Tanakh," [On-line], URL: http://www.hebrew4christians.com/Names_of_G-d/Messiah/messiah.html.

Pliny (no date), *Letters*, [On-line], URL: http://artemis.austincollege.edu/acad/hwc22/Rome/Pagans_v_Christians/Pliny_to_Trajan.html.

Polycarp (no date), *Epistle to the Philippians*, [On-line], URL: http://www.newadvent.org/fathers/0136.htm.

Price, Reynolds (1999), "Jesus of Nazareth–Then and Now," *Time*, 154[23]:84-94, December 6.

Rajak, Tessa (1984), *Josephus: The Historian and His Society* (Philadelphia, PA: Fortress).

Ramm, Bernard (1953), *Protestant Christian Evidences* (Chicago, IL: Moody).

Ramsay, William (1908), *Luke the Physician, and Other Studies in the History of Religion* (London: Hodder and Stoughton).

Ramsay, William (1915), *The Bearing of Recent Discovery on the Trustworthiness of the New Testament* (London: Hodder and Stoughton).

Ramsay, William (1915), *The Bearing of Recent Discovery on the Trustworthiness of the New Testament* (Grand Rapids, MI: Baker, 1975 reprint).

Renan, Ernest (no date), *Life of Jesus*, [On-line], URL: http://www.lexilogos.com/document/renan/life_jesus_28.htm.

Robertson, A.T. (1930), *Word Pictures in the New Testament,* (Nashville, TN: Broadman).

Robertson, A.T. (1932), *Word Pictures in the New Testament,* (Nashville, TN: Broadman).

Robertson, A.T. (1997), *Robertson's Word Pictures in the New Testament* (Electronic Database: Biblesoft).

Sagan, Carl (1980), *Cosmos* (New York: Random House).

Sanders, E.P. (1993), *The Historical Figure of Jesus* (New York, NY: Lane-Penguin).

Santala, Risto (1992), *The Messiah in the Old Testament: In the Light of Rabbinical Writings*, trans. William Kinnaird (Jerusalem, Israel: Keren Ahvah Meshihit).

Schaff, Philip (1913), *The Person of Christ: The Miracle of History* (New York: American Tract Society).

Schonfield, Hugh J. (1965), *The Passover Plot* (New York, NY: Bantam).

Shachter, Jacob, trans. (1994), *The Babylonian Talmud: Sanhedrin Tractate* (London: Soncino Press).

Smith, James (1993), *What the Bible Teaches about the Promised Messiah* (Nashville, TN: Thomas Nelson).

Stenning, John F. (1911), "Targum," *Encyclopedia Britannica*, eleventh edition. [On-line], URL: http://www.bible-researcher.com/aramaic3.html.

Stott, John (1971), *Basic Christianity* (Downers Groves, IL: InterVarsity Press).

Strobel, Lee (1998), *The Case for Christ* (Grand Rapids, MI: Zondervan).

Strong, A.H. (1907), *Systematic Theology* (Old Tappan, NJ: Fleming H. Revell).

Suetonius (1957 reprint), *The Twelve Caesars*, trans. Robert Graves (London: Penguin).

Tacitus, Cornelius P. (1952 reprint), *The Annals and the Histories*, trans. Michael Grant (Chicago, IL: William Benton), Great Books of the Western World Series.

Templeton, Charles (1996), *Farewell to God* (Ontario, Canada: McClelland and Stewart).

Tertullian (no date), *Apology*, [On-line], URL: http://www.newadvent.org/fathers/0301.htm.

Thompson, Bert (1994), "Famous Enemies of Christ–Ancient and Modern," *Reason & Revelation*, 14:1-7, January.

Thompson, Bert (2001), *In Defense of the Bible's Inspiration* (Montgomery, AL: Apologetics Press), second edition.

Thompson, Bert (2003), *The Case for the Existence of God* (Montgomery, AL: Apologetics Press).

Till, Farrell and Norman L. Geisler (1994), "Did Jesus of Nazareth Bodily Rise from the Dead?", [On-line], URL: http://www.infidels.org/library/modern/farrell_till/geisler-till/index.shtml.

Toledoth Yeshu (no date), [On-line], URL: http://ccat.sas.upenn.edu/humm/Topics/JewishJesus/toledoth.html.

Trench, R.C. (no date), *Christ the Desire of All Nations; or the Unconscious Prophecies of Heathendom* (Searcy, AR: Bales Publications).

Unger, Merrill (1962), *Archaeology and the New Testament* (Grand Rapids, MI: Zondervan).

Vincent, Marvin R. (1997), *Word Studies in the New Testament* (Electronic Database: Biblesoft).

Wells, H.G. (1931), *Outline of History, Being a Plain History of Life and Mankind* (Garden City, NY: Garden City Publishing).

Wells, Steve (2001), *The Skeptic's Annotated Bible*, [On-line], URL: http://www.Skepticsannotatedbible.com.

Welte, Michael (2005), personal e-mail to Dave Miller, Institute for New Testament Textual Research (Munster, Germany), [On-line], URL: http://www.uni-muenster.de/NTTextforschung/.

Wheeler, Lee S. (1931), *Famous Infidels Who Found Christ* (Peekskill, NY: Review and Herald Publishing).

Wilson, Edward O. (1978), *On Human Nature* (Cambridge, MA: Harvard University Press).

Witmer, John (1973), "The Doctrine of Miracles," *Bibliotheca Sacra*, 130:126-134, April.

Woodward, Kenneth L. (1999), "2000 Years of Jesus," *Newsweek*, 133[13]:52-63, March 29.

Woodward, Kenneth L. (2000), "The Other Jesus," *Newsweek*, 135[13]:50-60, March 27.

Wycliffe Bible Commentary (1985), Electronic Database: Biblesoft.

Yamauchi, Edwin M. (1995), "Jesus Outside the New Testament: What is the Evidence?," *Jesus Under Fire*, ed. Michael J. Wilkins and J.P. Moreland (Grand Rapids, MI: Zondervan).

Zerr, E.M. (1952), *Bible Commentary* (Raytown, MO: Reprint Publications).

Zomberg, Don (2000), "Letter to the Editor," *Newsweek*, 135[16]: 17, April 10.